RAGAMUFFIN
☀ RISING ☀

A Quiet Defiance of Small Town Norms

By Sandy Blais

Ragamuffin Rising
Copyright © 2021 Sandy Blais

ISBN: 978-1-954517-13-4

Designed and produced by:
Indie Author Books
12 High Street, Thomaston, Maine
www.indieauthorbooks.com

Printed in the United States of America

I dedicate this book to my children. I hope that I showed my love every day and was a lioness for you when needed. Also, to all the exceptional teachers that encourage every student to follow their dreams.

☙ ONE VERSION, ONE PERSPECTIVE ❧

I have no regrets, as I have lived the life I chose, in spite of being encouraged to live a different life. My sisters would tell a slightly different story. My parents were not aware of much of my story. Other families growing up in my small town would tell the same story, but from a much different perspective. I have sadness only for the children who listened and were convinced there was only one life to live. My story doesn't suggest that depression, resentment, or unhappiness is the result of my childhood; in fact, I feel just the opposite. Independence, resilience, strength, and the determination to be just what I wanted to be—that was the result of my childhood challenges. It was a different time, with social norms that tried to lock children into being what was expected based on their parents' education and economic status. Not all of us listened!

There may be some inconsistencies in my record of events, but they are as I remember them. Some of the time frames may be inaccurate, but the events did happen. The flashbacks of my parents were from stories told to me by my relatives as well as those related directly by my mother. I include these flashbacks so that the reader can gain some understanding, just as I have, of why my parents were the parents they were. I was told little of my father's childhood, although my grandfather, Pépère, shared other early stories with me. My mother and my uncle, her brother, were both afflicted with Alzheimer's in their late seventies. During those times, the most accurate stories of their youth emerged. They had both regressed into their own childhoods, often expressing the words and emotions of the most fearsome and sad moments of their early years. Only as an adult and caretaker did I truly have the gift of first person accounts of my mother's childhood. I wished the happier moments were a greater part of the memory she had left, but that is not often the way of Alzheimer's.

⚘ BEGINNINGS ⚘

My mom had always told me that her father had been born in the Parson-Capen House in Topsfield, Massachusetts. The official documentation of his birth says he was born in Ipswich, Massachusetts. His first wife died very young, without bearing any children. He bought a huge and beautiful gravestone for her and had a poem engraved on it. It is located in the Village Cemetery in Weymouth, Massachusetts. Henry worked his younger years as a butcher in Somerville, just outside of Boston. His second wife, Katherine Wipfler, was the daughter of a couple who came over in a boat; they emigrated from Germany. Kate, as Henry called her, lived in Somerville and liked city life. Henry wanted to farm, so he obtained a lease on land in Ipswich with a house his family would reside in. Kate and Henry had a son, Edward, and a few years later a daughter, Ruth. They raised hundreds of rabbits, selling them for food. Henry also farmed many acres of vegetables; as a tenant farmer, his crops were sold in Boston, with the landowner getting much of the profit. When the Depression hit, they lost the lease and had to move into an apartment on the hill just above downtown Ipswich. My aunt tells me that Henry died on the farm before they moved to the apartment. She says he did have high blood pressure, according to his son. Edward enlisted when he turned eighteen, having worked at Robertson's Shipyard in Ipswich and also at Marini Farm. Ruth worked at Sylvania in Ipswich.

My Mother's Family

Henry Perkins Andrews married Kate Wipfler
Children, Edward and Ruth

Edward married Delores Fortin
Children, Nancy and Dana

Ruth married Antonio Blais
Children, Patsy, Sandy, Jeanne, Janet

My Father's Family

Wilfred Blais married Marie Belanger
Children, Leopold and Antonio (my dad was also known as Mike or Tony)

Leopold married Opal Yerta
Children: Julie, Carol, Georgette, Joan, Roger, Linda, Denise, Richard,
John, Valerie, James

Antonio married Ruth Andrews
Children: Patsy, Sandy, Jeanne, Janet

On the gravestone Henry had made when his first wife died very shortly
after they were married, he had engraved:

> Just as the morning of her life was opening into day,
> Her young and lovely spirit passed from earth and grief away.

❧ FINALLY, CHILDREN! ☙

My mother tried for several years to get pregnant. My mom was taking care of a foster child at the time and she and my father were considering adoption if she didn't get pregnant soon. An "adoption lady," as she was described to me, came out to discuss what type of child they wanted. Calling my cousin Julie upstairs, my mom said, "I want one just like her." Julie was my aunt and uncle's oldest daughter, and she was a smart and beautiful little girl. My mom often repeated what the lady answered: "You sure are expecting a lot, aren't you?" They already were caring for a foster child, Kathy, and were getting attached to her; my mother always spoke fondly of her, even years later. From a picture that my mom kept, I thought Kathy did look a lot like Julie! During this time, my mom was experiencing vague pains that her doctor couldn't quite figure out. She had pains in her stomach, so they took out her appendix, and when she continued to have pains, they took out one ovary. Mom told me the doctor's medical diagnosis was "the ovary was rotten." I asked her many times to clarify, but she said that is what the doctor told her. She explained that the doctors didn't think women would understand complicated terms, so he must have just made it simple for her. Ironically, once the ovary was out, she soon became pregnant. I was a bit disappointed when she told me that they'd returned Kathy, their foster child, to Catholic Charities, but my mom didn't appear to think that this was a big deal. She did mention once that my father really wanted his "own" children. I truly believe my father had a much bigger influence on the decision to return Kathy than my mother did. However, as it became ever more apparent over the years, my mother did not assert herself with my father very often.

After Patsy was born, it wasn't long before my mom was pregnant again. I was born Sandra Marie Blais in the year 1952 in Beverly Hospital. My birth certificate states that I was born to Antonio Blais, game maker, and Ruth Andrews Blais, homemaker. Fifteen months after Patsy was born, there were two babies for mom to care for. My parents didn't have time to indulge in cooing and cuddling, because not only was my dad often working two jobs, my Nana had to move in with us. My mother's mom was in the beginning stages of dementia. Nana was a very tall, large woman with rather stern facial features. My mother revealed to me that her mom was never affectionate to her when she was a child, and I don't remember things changing much in terms of her demeanor toward us grandchildren. I know so many people who were the gruffest parents to their children but turned into sweet marshmallows with their grandchildren. Not so Nana! The agreement was that Uncle Eddie, my mother's brother, would share the caretaking and, although it started out that way, as her condition worsened, Aunt Doe and Uncle Eddie didn't feel they were capable of caring for Nana. In the early years, my grandmother may have actually been a help to my mother, at least as another set of eyes to watch over us. But it wasn't very long before dementia made the full-time care of Nana another burden on my mom, in addition to living conditions that were exhausting.

I must make a note that, although new work-saving devices were filling the homes of "modern" families in the fifties, we were living more like people did in the early forties. Farm life was a lot of work, even though we technically didn't run the farm. My dad's role was to keep everything in the huge old farmhouse working, in addition to his full-time job at the Parker Brothers games factory and weekend work hauling gravel and working sawmills. Keeping the farmhouse working included maintaining a wood-fired boiler in a basement far below the house that needed constant attention. What seemed like miles of pipes had to be prevented from freezing during the winter. The radiators had to be frequently "bled," another term for letting off steam so that the water could fill the radiator more fully. The heating system was from an earlier time, but we were lucky that we had town water! My mom had an old wringer washing machine in the house. She also had the longest pulley clothesline I have ever seen coming off the back porch, adjacent to a steep three-story set of stairs. The upstairs living quarters of the farmhouse had enough bedrooms that Nana had her own room and Patsy and I had our own rooms. That was until the twins came along.

The twins were born within three years of Patsy and me. Mom's family now included four girls, all under the age of four, one grandmother, and one father who was a traditional male of the 1940s. By traditional, I mean he made a clear distinction between women's work and his job of earning a paycheck and keeping us all warm and safe. Our dad also worked some night shifts in a mill when we had a house full of babies. Maybe he figured he wasn't going to get much sleep at home! With a fifth-grade education, he made what was considered a good day's wage at Parker Brothers in Salem, where many of the French-Canadian immigrants worked. However, it was never enough to support his growing family and pay the mortgage and taxes on the farm. He had bought the farm with his brother, Leopold. Although the payments were supposed to be equally shared between them, my father would never argue with his brother, because he would turn violent—and my father detested conflict. My father firmly believed in paying all his bills on time and he constantly worried about everything his brother wasn't worrying about at all! My father worked very hard but never at women's work! My mother often laughed when telling us about when she came home from the hospital with the twins. Her amazement at the clean counters, without a dirty dish in sight, turned into disbelief when she opened the oven to cook a meal. My father had stacked all the dirty dishes in the oven while she was at the hospital!

Just a note must be included here. There was no planning for twins in our home, as the doctor dismissed my mother's insistence that "there was way too much kicking for one baby." In those days, there was no ultrasound or finding out the sex of your baby before the child was born. And evidently there also wasn't very much respect or consideration of a woman's knowledge of her own body, even if she had already birthed two children. For the first two deliveries, me and Patsy, my mom said she was "knocked out cold," evidently meaning she was heavily sedated. She "never felt a thing," and that was fine with her. Just a few years later, they must have given only light sedatives, because she was very aware of having birthed one of the twins and just knowing the other one was still in there. She said she heard the nurse yell to the doctor, "We got another baby in there," and then, sure enough, another little girl was born!

Two infants, two toddlers, a mother with dementia, and a husband who expected his Cream of Wheat every morning without lumps was just too much for my mom. She told me that after a few months she had what she described as a "nervous breakdown." That must have been the term for total exhaustion in the fifties! She actually spent a few days in the hospital to rest and returned to the same rigors of farm life, but with renewed determination. My mom often said that her sister-in-law downstairs had it so hard that she never felt she should complain. My Aunt Opal was from tough stock and was married to an even tougher man with a temper. My mom always wondered if Opal had it rough growing up in Alabama with part Native American ancestry. In the South, during times of much racial tension and class distinction, women surely had a more difficult time than those in the North. Aunt Opal had also enlisted and served our country as a WAC during World War II; this is where she had met my uncle. Aunt Opal was very beautiful, shapely, intelligent, and strong. She also was a dedicated mother and would never leave her young children behind to escape such a hard life. My father said it was not our business what went on between a wife and her husband. Aunt Opal handled the rigorous farm life without complaint, milking the cows daily and raising eleven children. My mom felt she should be able to raise just four daughters! She would have been right, except for the presence of Nana.

Nana wouldn't keep her clothes on. I was a toddler—my mom was amazed that I remembered so much from when I was so young. There are some things that you can never erase from your memory. Nana had lost a lot of weight, as if all the air had been let out of a balloon. She just deflated. The sight before my eyes, which were about three feet off the floor, was wrinkle after wrinkle of flesh, none of it being where it had started. Her stomach was almost knee level, right in front of my face. If I looked up, I couldn't see past the pendulous breasts hanging to her waist. If she walked away from me, her buttocks sagged almost to her knees, all of this skin being just wrinkles and more wrinkles. I am not intending to be disrespectful, but a child shouldn't have to see such a thing. And she wouldn't keep her clothes on! My mom screamed and yelled at Nana all day, but every time she got her dressed again, Nana would strip naked within a few minutes and walk around the house. Some days were not as bad as others and I have a few pictures with my Nana in which she appears grandmotherly. Those were very rare occasions. The next thing to happen was incontinence, and that was when life really changed in our house!

Can you imagine having three kids and an elderly mother, all of whom wet their beds every single night? Patsy was the oldest and the only child who went from diapers to staying dry at night. She must have inherited the only normal-size bladder! Even with rubber sheets protecting the mattress, all the bottom sheets, and sometimes the top sheets, too, had to be laundered daily. The old washing machine went nonstop every morning, threatening to take my mom's hand off in the wringer. She then had to hang the sheets outside on the clothesline while standing at the top of a three-story outdoor staircase, bring them in after they were dry, and fold them up to be used again in just a few days, as we didn't have many extra sets of sheets. Often the blankets had to be washed too! This was in addition to the regular laundry that four toddlers, an elderly woman, and a laboring man dirtied each day!

I have never disliked a word so much. For my entire life, I forbade anybody to use this word in my presence, regardless of what they referred to. My ears still curl over, and I cringe inside. The word is "piss," as Mom screamed it, "pissy sheets," "pissy beds," and "pissy pajamas." That one adjective haunts me to this day. It wasn't a short period of time that this word was yelled by my mom every single morning when confronted with those wet sheets. It lasted my entire early childhood and into my early school years, as my younger sisters wet the bed for many years. I, myself, wet the bed until my problem was solved the Christmas I was four. In my defense and that of my two younger twin sisters, apparently, we inherited small bladders from my father. He once told the story—or more likely I overheard him telling my mom—about his bed-wetting problem. He was actually thrown out of his Army barracks, wet mattress and all, by the other soldiers. He says it was the last time he wet the bed, but I would venture that he also never got a good night's sleep while in the Army!

In contrast to today's homes with many bathrooms, our huge farmhouse had one bathroom on the upstairs level where our family lived. It was at the end of the long procession of rooms adjacent to the gigantic, long kitchen. For us children to get to the bathroom in the night, we had to walk from our room through another bedroom, down a hallway, and then through the living room. It was a long, dark walk, and my frugal father would never consider, or allow, a light to be left on, not even a small nightlight. So although I wasn't capable of "holding it" all night, I must have been awake when I peed in my bed when I was almost four years old. Because then a miracle occurred! Santa Claus gave me a little red battery lantern that Christmas. From that point on, I never wet my bed! Off I went, walking in the light of my trusty lantern, to the bathroom several times during the night; however, it wasn't as easy for my younger sisters.

Jeanne and Janet didn't just have small bladders, they were also heavy sleepers. They never woke in the night and their bed-wetting continued for years, even after we moved into a smaller, ranch-style house. And my mom continued yelling about "pissy" sheets every morning for hours. She could use the word "piss" in so many ways it was absolutely amazing. Sometimes she would use it three for four times in one sentence! My sisters seemed okay when they were very young, but as they got to be older, they became aware that everybody got to see their sheets drying on the clothesline every day. My mom was so frustrated, tired, and seemingly angry at the situation, she didn't ever consider how shaming a child could have some serious emotional effects on her. Thank goodness the twins had each other for comfort. Even though I was glad she wasn't yelling at me anymore, the constant yelling was very upsetting. Me, I never stopped sleeping with my trusty little lantern!

The Blais farmhouse, we lived upstairs and my uncle's family lived downstairs, was designed with the bedrooms on the far right and the one bathroom far away on the far left to the rear of the kitchen. It was a long walk to the bathroom at night, a trek we did not make very often.

My mom cared for her mother, Nana to us, and my sisters and I. I don't remember Nana ever laughing.

11

❧ TODDLER ROAD TRIP ❧

My mother used to ask me, when I was older, "How can you remember those things, you were only two years old?" I believe it was the multi-sensory aspects of each experience that cemented them into my memory. The power of smell seems to be the greatest elicitor of memory for me, followed by visuals that I will never forget. The trip to Kentucky to visit old friends, the Sidebottoms, was the first road trip for Patsy and me; the twins had not yet been born. We were headed for the country, what I would now describe as the "mountain hollers" of Appalachia.

My first vivid memory was of breakfast in a cow pasture. I can smell the morning dew on the grass and the cows grazing just inside the fence. We had very little money, and it was a splurge just to take this drive, so we did not have the funds to eat at restaurants along the way. As a two-year-old, I didn't know what state we were in by breakfast time, but it was a great place to eat. Mom had packed a cooler with our food. On this morning, we were having cereal in individual one-serving boxes that were evidently wax coated to hold milk for a short time. After my mom cut on the dotted line to make an opening in the top and poured the milk in, I enjoyed the treat of a sugary cereal all to myself. Later, as I related that pleasure to my mom, asking to have little boxes of cereal again, she was astonished that I remembered such details. She said it was the only time we had done that! I also vividly remember getting to my parents' friend's cabin home. My mom helped me walk on a rope footbridge traversing a gorge. The damp smells of forest and water, the wobbly bridge—it was very memorable and fun for me!

Unfortunately, that was our one and only visit to a primitive cabin in the Kentucky "hollers"! Many years later we visited again, but the Sidebottoms had moved to the suburbs of Louisville, into a very nice but boring neighborhood of small, cookie-cutter homes. My older sister did not remember any of the earlier car trip. My mom said that Patsy could not walk for a few days after the ride home. I don't remember stopping once on the return trip. Mom took her to the doctor and was told that it was a temporary condition caused by too many hours sitting in the car. Maybe Patsy, at three years old, had not enjoyed the trip as much as I had and did not want to remember it. After all, I was used to sitting in the playpen for hours, just talking to myself and observing, while Patsy was riding in dump trucks and having fun with Dad during her early years.

❧ MOM'S FLASHBACK TO 1954, IN HER WORDS ❧

"**D**addy, Daddy, Daddy," Sandy cried as she watched Mike lift Patsy up into the front seat of the dump truck. With her face pressed against the window, she stayed there until the dump truck drove away, heading for the gravel pit to load some gravel his brother needed on a job. She was in her playpen when I dressed Patsy for the cold. Sandy spent most of all her early years in her playpen, chattering to herself and imitating the adults she listened to. She didn't have very good physical skills, not like Patsy. Patsy wouldn't stay in the playpen; she started climbing and walking very quickly, although she hardly ever talked. Mike was happy to take Patsy with him; he took her every day that he wasn't working at the factory. Patsy could run around where he was working and she hardly talked, so she was good company for Mike. I couldn't stand listening to Sandy's crying at home very much longer. She would cry so much to go with Mike that she would wake the babies and upset my mother. Now that she was finally walking, she would go from window to window, hoping to spot them coming home to get her. They never did. It wasn't fair, I knew that. I also knew it wouldn't stop if I didn't say something.

That evening, after a long day of Sandy crying off and on for her daddy, I told Mike that it wasn't fair. Sandy really wanted a turn to go with him in the truck and on jobs on the weekend. He would have to take them both. Mike was quiet for a long time, but finally he said, "If I can't take just Patsy, I won't take either of them. I can't handle two kids while I am working." He wouldn't consider one at a time. Maybe he had visions of Sandy talking to him all day.

The next time Mike had a job with the dump truck, Patsy scrambled to get ready. Mike said to her, "Your mother says I have to take Sandy, too, and I can't take two kids, so you can't come." Patsy didn't cry. She just looked at Sandy like she wanted to kill her all day long. They sometimes played together, but there seemed to be a lot more injuries when they played together from that day on. Sandy was safer in the playpen.

MOM SPEAKS OF HER CHILDHOOD

"Hundreds and hundreds of rabbits. Every day, hours of cleaning out cages. Don't ever pet them or make one into a pet, 'these are eating rabbits,' my dad would say. Eddie and I couldn't stand this job. And I never want to eat rabbit again, ever!"

⚶ TOO MANY CATS ⚶

When we lived upstairs in the Blais farmhouse, we had a lot of cats. My cousin Carol recently shared that her most vivid memory was of my mom constantly calling for her cats from the top of the back staircase. We loved our cats but, back in the early fifties, we didn't have money to have the females spayed. Not very many people did, and it was not considered irresponsible until many years later. However, upsetting as it was to me, it was common knowledge that some people got rid of animals in cruel ways. My mother stressed to us that she could never do this but did tell us children that a woman who lived across town was known as the "drowning lady." I'm not sure if it was a threat to us not to "adopt" any more stray cats than we already had or just a reflection on life, but I could never look that woman in the eye when we went to her house to visit, which, thankfully, wasn't often. Every little town had an egg lady and a milkman, but we also had a person performing the service of drowning cats. We never used her services, but that wasn't to say we didn't have too many cats.

One week, the milkman not only fulfilled his milk delivery service, but he also took care of the cat problem. I can still visualize the carnage. My sister and I were sitting on the bottom steps of our back stairway when the milk truck pulled around behind the house. My cousins drank the milk directly from the cow, unpasteurized, but we didn't own the cows, and my mom and dad liked bottled milk. We had the same milkman for years, a round-bellied jovial man in overalls. My mom joked easily with him, and he always had friendly comments for all the kids running around the yard. Up until "that day," we really liked him. We were playing with the youngest batch of kittens, laughing at their antics as they frolicked in the yard. We saw the milk truck pulling around into the back yard and we all started yelling for him to watch out for our kittens. He couldn't hear us, and we watched in horror as the wide tires mushed several of our cute little kittens as he pulled in and parked. They weren't crushed or bumped; they were mushed into bloody blobs in the dirt. We cried and screamed in horror and my mother ran out the door to witness us turning our anger on the milkman. Mom said that the milkman was never the same. Every time he brought the milk from that day on, he looked distraught and uncomfortable as we just stared at him with accusing eyes.

ᘏ MY COUSIN JULIE WAS FAMOUS! ᘏ

I still have an old, tattered copy of a front-page story in the *Salem News*, the largest newspaper that delivered to Middleton. My mom had saved it for years! The headline was "JULIE BLAIS MASTERS T.D. 18," with the subtitle "Nine-year-old Middleton Girl Handles Controls of Bulldozer and Other Mechanical Equipment." It really caught the reader's attention. The writer goes on to explain that most girls would be playing with dolls and would shy away from bulldozers and hay balers. It also states, "While her father is at work, Julie carries on the business of loading loam when a customer calls for it." The article also tells of Julie running the hay baler as well as other farm equipment. At the time, Julie, the youngest of ten, eventually to be eleven, was also described as a beautiful child, which was very true! The article also conveyed that she had been running heavy equipment since she was five years old, which was also true. The story was written in July, so most readers probably assumed Julie did this work only while she was off school for the summer. They would be wrong. Most readers probably also assumed Julie loved doing this work, which she may have, but she also did not have a choice.

The one thing the writer did not do was ask Julie any questions—or at least print any of her answers. For the record, my Uncle Paul, named Leopold at birth, told the authorities that all his children attended St. Joseph's Catholic school in Salem. And sometimes they did! My father drove them, as he worked in Salem at Parker Brothers. His car was rarely full, and there were a lot of Blais kids. I have always been disturbed that nobody questioned the safety of a child running heavy equipment while her father and mother were at work. Julie was the oldest child, so there was no older sibling to watch over her. This wasn't the forties, this was the fifties, and we didn't live off the grid, unknown to the world. A front-page article about a little girl from Haswell Park, right off busy Route 114, and nobody questioned the sanity of a parent that would allow this. Nobody questioned if that beautiful little girl had a choice about working so hard.

I am sure it was exciting. We all loved having the job as operator, as it was much easier than working the boring tasks on the ground. My father told us girls to "get up there and drive" when we were about nine or ten, but he was always nearby. And we only drove a farm tractor with a front bucket. We also knew that if we really didn't want to do something, we could cry and get a boring job on the ground instead. My uncle was much different. He worked his children to the bone, every day except Sunday! Most of them will tell you it made them strong women; I also feel my childhood made me a strong woman. However, my memories never included those of being forced to work. Some of my cousins still bear the pain of their childhood memories. Others rejoice that their father, once he was an elderly grandfather, was loved by his grandchildren.

JULIE BLAIS MASTERS, T. D. 18

Nine-Year-Old Middleton Girl Handles Controls of Bulldozer and Other Mechanical Equipment

Middleton, July 24—Most nine-year-old girls, in their spare time, gather their dolls around them and play "house."

Most nine-year-old youngsters, boy or girl, shy away from anything so menacing as a bulldozer or hay bailer.

Not so, Julie Blais, daughter of Mr. and Mrs. Leopold Blais of Haswell park, who at that tender age has mastered the technique of mechanism that often baffles teen-age boys and adults.

Since the age of five, Julie has spent most of her time riding around on tractors and such with her father.

She doesn't care much for dishes and dolls. But operating the machines has always fascinated her and has never been considered work.

While her father is at work, Julie carries on the business of loading loam when a customer calls for it. They are not only amazed but quite envious of the little girl who climbs into the seat of the T.D. 9 and fills their order with the ease and competence of an experienced operator.

Recently a new T.D. 18 a rived at the farm while father was at work and to amazement of the truck dri Julie ..nloaded it. She has assisted her father in hayin running the hay bailer.

Julie, the youngest of c ildren, is a beautiful brown-eyed girl, as swe feminine as any nine-y should be, and it hard that she has accor much in such a few

My cousin Julie was highlighted on the front page of the Salem News, *one of the two largest newspapers in the area. I found this tattered copy in my mother's cherished things, she adored Julie.*

☀ ACCIDENTS HAPPEN ☀

The Blais farm was messy. Most farms in which the owners had to work a variety of other jobs to pay the bills were. My uncle worked for the Middleton DPW but also ran gravel trucks and did excavating jobs. There was a large garage for working on trucks, and next to the garage was an old drive-up car lift. Because it was no longer being used to lift cars so mechanics could work under them, the area under it became the spot where junk was thrown. However, my cousins and my sisters liked to play King of the Hill on top of it, pushing each other off. It is crucial to remember that all the adults were too busy working to monitor what we little kids were doing.

That day while we were playing, my younger sister, Jeanne, took a shove and wasn't able to catch herself on the car lift, falling full weight on a broken ceramic toilet bowl. She was only about four years old. With all the screaming we did, the adults came running. My mother depended a lot on the Nelson family, who rented a small house on the farm, as Janet Nelson was a registered nurse. Her husband, Peter, scooped Jeanne up in his arms and almost made it to his car before taking a good look at the injury and proceeding to get sick. It was incredibly grotesque. An entire block of flesh, right to the bone of her leg, was cut out of her thigh, connected only on one side by skin. My mother took one look and almost passed out. Thank goodness my dad was just pulling in the driveway from work and immediately took action. He carried her to his car and raced off to the hospital.

Jeanne remembers the doctor in the emergency room of the hospital being rude and yelling at her to stop crying. My normally quiet father started yelling at him that she was only four years old and he could show some sympathy. That, or because he was incompetent with stitches, is why the Hunt Hospital emergency room doctor did such a butcher job of stitching her leg. To this day, Jeanne has a humongous scar filling her entire thigh area! Not surprisingly, we were not allowed to play on the car rack over the junk pile anymore.

❧ I MIGHT HAVE HAD A BROTHER ❧

I was told the story many times. I only knew at the time that I was sent to my godmother's house for a few days and my sisters went someplace else. And after my mother got out of the hospital, we sold Dusty.

Our first horse, Dusty, was just a pony. Dad got ripped off. The Bundletts said he was a great beginner horse for younger children, and we paid good money for him, but Dusty was not a good pony for anybody. He was a good-looking Shetland pony with a beautiful mane and tail. However, we found out quickly that he could be mean and ornery. The only way we could ride him was with Dad tightly holding the reins at all times. Dad had to hold him even when we just wanted to brush him. It wasn't a lot of fun.

Mom was pregnant but she wasn't sharing that with many people. Her doctor had told her she was too old when she had the twins in her late thirties, and she was almost forty now. The doctor would have preferred to talk to my father, as was the practice in the early fifties, but my father refused to go with Mom to the doctor's. He was especially reluctant when it involved women's personal body concerns. Mom's pregnancy didn't show very much because she was so active that she wasn't gaining much weight. Her farm dresses hid a lot too. She went out to feed Dusty in his stall, and as she passed behind him, he got out a long and hard kick. It went right to her lower abdomen. Mom told me that, "I felt a snap inside me and knew that cord had ripped loose." Pain enveloped her but she made it upstairs and to her bed. For years, she told me often, "I couldn't call the doctor, he would just yell at me for walking behind a horse when I was pregnant." She somehow got us kids through supper and off to bed early even though she had started bleeding almost immediately after the kick. She soaked through huge pads. When my father got home, he had her stay in bed, but the bleeding only became heavier. She was adamant he not call the doctor. He put newspapers under her and ran them down to the boiler after they were soaked in blood. Mom said he was getting more and more upset. He yelled, "I am not making one more trip to that boiler." He finally couldn't take it anymore. Mom remembered and shared all the details with me many times, even when I was a pre-teen. She continued her story with what Dad did to save her life. Our father called somebody from downstairs to stay with us kids and, with Mom almost unconscious, he carried her to the car and drove her to the hospital. She had lost a lot of blood and was admitted immediately.

Years later, she told me she was relieved that "the doctors never asked if anything had happened, they just said I was so old that miscarriages happen a lot." I believe at the time my mother was almost forty years of age! She was always very specific when she told me the story, and she told it over and over. Dad never spoke of it. She and I always wondered if it would have finally been a boy. The details never left her, and neither did the guilt.

⚡ OUR NEW HOUSE ⚡

I was almost six years old and had a very important job! I was to bring the carpenters, who were building my new house, cold drinks on the hot summer days. My older sister and I had already helped my dad spread tar all over the cement block foundation. We used an old straw broom, and that tar was hot and heavy. We had to cover the cement blocks up to where the backfill would go. We didn't mind the job and my father didn't have to force us; yucky jobs were actually fun. But my next job was easier.

One of the carpenters had a gold tooth, which was something I had never seen before. I believed he worked for Bill Cashman, a local builder who would, many years later, become the building inspector for the town. When I brought jugs of water from the old Blais farmhouse, the workers smiled and thanked me. I remember the carpenter sitting up on the roof in the hot sun, how the sun glinted off his tooth when he smiled. I loved making people happy and loved my water delivery job!

This home would be just for us. Because Nana had become too much to care for, my mother had to put her in the nursing home section of Danvers State Hospital. Mom always clarified that it was the "nursing" section of the hospital. Nana was not a mentally ill or violent patient, those Danvers State Hospital was primarily built for in the 1800s. A separate building housed elderly people with dementia. My mom visited her almost every day and came home upset that they just couldn't seem to keep socks on Nana. She almost cried about her mother having cold feet, and had such guilt about having to leave her there. Nana passed

26

away at the facility. Mom spoke often of how she wished she had never placed her in that place. I tried to remind her that she had four young children to care for and couldn't lift Nana anymore. Guilt, however, was a part of my mother's character that could never be relieved.

As for us children, we were so happy that we were going to have three bedrooms in our new house, two of us in each of two rooms and one a bit farther down the hall for our parents. The bedrooms were very small, so we had bunk beds in each room, with Patsy and I in one room and Jeanne and Janet together in the other bedroom. We had a nice kitchen, a small dining room, living room, and one bathroom. The kitchen had a propane gas stove and sort of an island with a countertop that looked like floor linoleum. The washing machine was in the cellar, along with the exceptional heating system my father installed himself. To avoid confusion, our cellar would now be called the "basement," but as it was cement block walls and unfinished, we always called it a cellar. Also, my mother didn't like us using what she called "rich people's words." We had a wood-fired boiler (with back-up oil, he said, in case he ever got sick) that heated a huge tank of hot water. The hot water was both for the radiators and for baths. The bulkhead, pronounced "bow-ked" by my parents and hence by us, opened into the cellar from the outside, making it efficient to cut the firewood and heave it into the cellar. We had a dry well for the washing machine and a regular septic system behind the house. Our house had town water just as the big farmhouse did. I think our mortgage was about $18,000. It was a very small ranch home, and my father completed all the finish work himself. This was a lot of money for a factory worker, yet my father had one serious priority. He spent an exorbitant amount of money on a fully hard-wired fire alarm system for our house. After years of worry about fire in the big farmhouse, he had a much greater concern about house fires than most people of the day. I believe even in larger, more expensive homes of the day, the stick-on battery alarms were the norm. As Dad never shared deep emotional thoughts, we never knew, when we were younger, if he had other reasons to be very afraid of fires. Maybe he just wanted to get a good night's sleep for the first time in his married life. My father was so proud and my mother so relaxed with the prospect of having a house all to ourselves.

Our house was down the street and on the opposite side from the big Blais farmhouse. Our backyard abutted a swamp that drained out to a pond on my uncle's land. Across the street we owned a small pasture with the Richardson family cemetery in the middle, then nice woodlands, eventually going down into a cranberry bog. When my Uncle Paul split the land with my father, we got mostly wetlands with just a few high areas for the house and an area near the opposite side of the street for working wood and having cookouts. The good part was that there were trails from our woods that went all the way to my grandfather's house, way up on Route 114, the major road through town.

We had fun during every season outside our smaller new house. My mom always made us dress in many layers in the winter, and then we would itch when we went indoors to 80 degree heat!

⚘ MUD PIES ⚘

No soil upon Earth
Is so dear to our eyes
As the soil we first stirred in
Terrestrial pies.
—Oliver Wendell Holmes

There is nothing more rewarding to the senses than making mud pies. We would start by collecting tin pie plates, spoons, and a myriad of natural decorations. We knew we could go to the pile of wrappings from the thrift bakery pile, the ones we would unwrap to feed the cows. The pie tins, both small individual and full-size, were just perfect. We would hope for a hot summer sun, as the pies needed to bake before we could sell them!

Finding the perfect loam, clean black dirt with a bit of clay, was a challenge. We didn't want gravel or sand; it didn't make for a nice pie. Usually, the best place to find it was near the garden we had close to the swamp. On hot summer days, when the swamp was low, you had to be careful of sticking your hands in a hole where the big black snakes might be resting. After getting a big enough bucketful so we each could make three or four pies, we would get to the fun part. Adding just the right amount of water to make it squishy and oozy, but not runny, we mixed it with our hands and spooned it into the pie plates very carefully. We only knew it was a lot of fun, not realizing this was sensory heaven!

After the mud set just enough so the decorations wouldn't sink, we'd summon our greatest creativity. I personally loved using daises, often using a few intact ones, but then trimming the edges of the pie with petals. Small stones, sticks, leaves, tiny pinecones, and anything else we could find in the woods or the fields, Mother Nature's creations, were incorporated into a pie design that was an artistic wonder, to us at least. Then we would let the sun bake them.

After they were completely dry, by mid-afternoon, we would load them on a flat wagon and peddle our creations. Nobody on the Blais farm ever bought them, even for five cents. We weren't discouraged. We traded them among ourselves or pretended to shop from each other. The pies were not allowed into the house anyway, as my mother constantly washed the floor and covered it with newspaper to keep it clean. She wasn't having mud in the house. After our forts were built, they would sit on the shelves in our fort kitchen, until we got old enough to make some real food there.

Later, as a teacher of children with multiple diagnoses, including sensory needs, I would remind the parents of all the free sensory activities their children could enjoy, if they just went outdoors. They chose expensive sensory therapy with a skilled therapist!

☀ WE CLEANED UP WELL! ☀

In the old farmhouse, we had a long counter next to the sink. We had the same set-up in our new house. This was how we got our hair washed: Until we were tall enough to stand and hang our head over the sink, it was great to just lie on the kitchen counter. Dropping our heads down into the sink, we rarely got soap in our eyes. Mom always put a rolled-up towel under our necks, too.

Once we were tall enough, even if it took a giant cooking pot for more elevation, we had to stand in front of the sink with head forward and eyes covered with hands. Patsy was so tall she went straight from the counter to standing on the floor. For a long time, the twins and I needed a pot to stand on. Even though baby shampoo was advertised not to sting, it really stung your eyes a lot. However, that was nothing compared to Mr. Bubble in the bathtub. Mom splurged on some for us, and it was fun in the tub, but for a long time after the bath, it stung viciously every time we had to pee. This might have just been a girl's thing, but we were all girls!

My mother was proud to have her girls clean and dressed nicely. Every Saturday night we had a bath and shampoo. With the wood boiler, a fire had to be made hours before expecting to have hot water. The tub was filled only about three inches, so our bottoms were warm but our upper halves were cold. Usually at least two kids had to bathe together. The bath water just one night a week was never enough to soften our hands. We all had calluses. The school nurse or a teacher reported this once and somebody from social services came out to visit us. My father

31

told them we could work just as well as any boys and it wasn't hurting us at all. We agreed! We did always hope the bath water would soak out the splinters. Mom was deadly with a needle. She seemed to take great satisfaction in digging a splinter out of our skin. We learned to keep our splinters to ourselves unless we wanted even more pain. Sometimes we would complain about physical ailments. Jeanne and Janet spent a few years with severe cracks in their feet and nothing was done to relieve their pain. I felt bad, but if you weren't severely bleeding and nothing was broken, nobody got to go to the doctor. We did get our shots, even a few extra tetanus shots due to lots of rusty cuts and puncture wounds. In comparison to today's children, we actually got only a few vaccines in our entire childhood. I don't remember getting the measles, but I do remember all of us getting the mumps. It was memorable because we got ice cream and frappes. We did get a polio vaccine, as there were people in town who had polio and suffered ill effects long after. My mother got along very well with the nurse for Dr. Jones, calling her by her first name, Norma. Yet we had all our yearly physicals by Dr. Wiswell at school. My mother loved free!

So we were bathed weekly and we had clean clothes to wear. Our clothes were not expensive, but they were in good repair. Mom had a sewing machine and could fix clothes, although she didn't make them. Patsy and I were usually dressed very practically. Mom loved to dress the twins, Jeanne and Janet, in matching outfits. We had a beautiful new outfit for Easter every year—one of the benefits of going to church on Sunday.

⚘ MOM COULD BE A LIONESS ⚘

When we lived upstairs in the huge Blais farmhouse, we spent a lot of time on the back stairway. As my cousins had to work so much and the younger kids would be so sad, my cousin Carol would sing to cheer everybody up. I have never forgotten her rendition of "High Hopes." "High apple pie in the skyyyyy hopes" still plays often in my head. I think she could have had a career in singing, she had such a beautiful voice.

My mom would often give us a treat of homemade popsicles on hot summer days. We would sit on the back steps that overlooked the farmyard. One day, my uncle started yelling up at us, "You are no better than my kids, get down here and work with them." My mother heard him, charged out onto the stoop, and screamed at him. "My kids are not your slaves and do not have to listen to you!" She then stood there all puffed up to her five foot two inches and glared at him. My mother stood up to her brother-in-law even though my father didn't, at least when it came to her children. "Frenchy," as he was then called, backed down and walked off, yelling at his own kids to get back to work. In a few more years, one of his daughters would attach a new derogatory name to him, one that we never used, but even some townspeople knew of (more on this later). My uncle didn't mellow out until he became a grandfather many years later, and his grandchildren have good memories of "Grampy."

⚜ MOM SPEAKS OF HER CHILDHOOD ⚜

Again, I've done something to anger my mother. It was always something. As usual, Eddie probably started it, but then again, he didn't mind spending most of the day locked in the cellar. That's because he didn't! Eddie wasn't afraid of spiders or the dark. After being sent into the basement, he waited until he heard Mom shuffle away from the door before he left me alone on the top step. I'd hear him climbing up old boxes, pushing the back cellar window open, and then a slight scraping as he slid out of our stuffy, cold, and dreadful cellar. Me, I just sat on the top step with my eyes fixed on the sliver of light that always shone under the door. Even if she forget about us until after dark, the light always shone, actually shining brighter when the kitchen bulbs replaced the natural sunlight. I was always amazed that Eddie returned before my mom decided to open the door and let us up into her world again.

Eventually, I started to get angry, and that anger gave me courage to face the cellar demons. Eddie had tried for months to get me to be brave enough to escape with him. This time he held my hand and led me through the dark cellar, pushed me up the box "staircase," and practically shoved me out into the sunlight. My days locked in that cellar were over, at least until we were caught! Ironically, that never happened, and I wonder if we were so far from my mom's mind that she really didn't care where we were, as long as it was out of her way.

🌿 AND FORMAL SCHOOL BEGINS! 🌿

My birthday was in October, meaning I would be able to start school before I turned six, the mandatory age to enter public school. There was no preschool or kindergarten in the fifties, at least not out in the country! My parents never had the time or inclination to read stories to us, feeling that formal schooling was the place for that. My father read the Sears catalog every night—he justified saving all the old ones by telling us often that they could be used as toilet paper if times ever got really bad! They were also great to use as booster seats when we were toddlers. My mother had an old Bible, but she brought it out only to record births, marriages, and deaths in it. My father taught us what he felt was important: life survival skills. My mother was so busy caring for her mother who had serious dementia, as well as four young children, that she had no time for teaching early academics. We spent much of our developing years in a playpen, where we learned to amuse ourselves. I had no problem with that, according to my mom. "You just sat there and chattered away all day," she often told me. After the playpen, I spent a lot of my time hiding under my mother's skirt. I was very shy when strangers came into the house when I was a toddler.

Patsy was so different from me. She was much more physically advanced than I was at the same age, yet she talked very little. Her personality was obviously much more like my father's! She could jump over the sides of the playpen when I was content to sit there! Mom could care for the twins and her mother knowing I would stay in the playpen and talk to myself. When the twins needed the playpen, they could entertain each other!

Patsy started school the year before me, but I don't remember her talking of the experience at all. That was probably for the best, because I had the same first grade teacher that she did. The Howe-Manning School had been enlarged just a few years before, so the first-grade classroom was spacious and had its own bathroom, a feature I was very pleased with. I can't visualize her face, but I can remember her harsh voice, her hitting students' hands with a ruler, and, most importantly, her not letting us use that bathroom when we needed to. It was only four feet from my desk. With the exception of Patsy, it seemed that we all had small bladders in my family, and I was only five years old until October. I was not able to hold it very long. I raised my hand and asked permission to use the bathroom very nicely, only to be told that I should have gone before class started. I asked again but was again told no. I tried and tried, but the urine just would not stop coming out once it started. The seat filled up and, humiliated, I sat in my chair as a huge puddle formed around me on the floor. I cried as all the children started pointing and whispering. I would have crawled under my desk to hide if the puddle wasn't there! I don't remember how I got to the office, but I do know that I was sent home in my wet clothes. It was an experience I have never forgotten.

An interesting twist to this event happened over thirty years later when I was working as a teacher in Middleton. My classroom, an integrated special needs class, was being moved to the original Howe-Manning School, and the superintendent personally showed me my room. It was my own original first-grade classroom! I walked in, glanced over to the very same bathroom only a few feet from where my desk had been so many years earlier, and said, "Let me tell you of my first-grade experience. Trauma like that never goes away in a child's mind." I could feel the humiliation as if it had just happened yesterday! Every teacher needs to know that just one horrific experience can impact a child's emotional development for life. Dr. Creeden listened intently and his face showed compassion and shock, but it didn't change the fact that this would be my classroom so many years later. I taught for a few years in that classroom until moving to the early childhood elementary school, Fuller Meadow. My preschool integrated special education classrooms always had a bathroom in the room; I would have insisted on that accommodation. My most important rule for my students has always been, "If you have to go, just GO!"

Both my sister, when she first entered school, and I a year later, were immediately placed in the lowest reading group. The lack of a literacy-rich home environment contributed to our inability to do tasks that assessed for placement. We could do all kinds of tough and challenging farm work, but we didn't even know how to hold a book the right way! My birth certificate listed my father's occupation as a factory worker. It was a small town, and we were poor. My father's fifth-grade education, as he'd had to leave school to start working with his father, and my mother's high school diploma were more damning background information. My mother did brag that you can get a high school diploma with all Cs, unaware that she wasn't impressing school administrators. Also, children were routinely judged by siblings and relatives that had previously attended the school. Patsy had not been able to impress her teacher. Yet, my parents had full confidence in "educated" people, leaving important decisions about our education to those that "know what is best for children."

Reading groups were the most important factor relevant to a child becoming a reader. Teachers were becoming more aware of not "labeling" groups with words and phrases such as "low," "dumb," or "worthy of my time." So, we had animal names! The one thing a farm kid knows is that turtles are a lot slower than foxes or horses. I spent my first-grade year with the turtles, and knew very well that I was in the "slow and dumb" group. Every child knew exactly what the animal names meant. As we were resilient and emotionally strong, that wasn't as important as the fact that reading never seemed like any fun. To listen to each member of the reading group read aloud was torture. Not that Dick and Sally was a plot to get excited about, but when most of us read, it didn't even sound like words. "RRRRRR, UUUUUUU, NNNNNNNN." I absolutely needed to run! Is it time for recess yet? The teacher spent most of her time with the Road Runners or Coyotes, and I don't blame her. I didn't act up though, as the teacher was allowed to rap your knuckles with that ruler! Jeesh, I had already peed on the floor. I didn't need the greater humiliation of being physically punished.

As if it wasn't bad enough to be really slow at reading letters, I apparently also had atrocious breath. The teacher reported this to my parents, who evidently didn't get as close to me as she did. After the peeing on the floor incident, my teacher may have felt a bit guilty and was a bit nicer. I think telling my parents I had horrid breath was doing me a favor. My mom took me to Dr. Jones, the only doctor in town, and his diagnosis was tonsillitis. There was a family special deal, as almost all children had their tonsils out as a child. It was either two for one or a reduced price, but only if the siblings go in together at the same time. Patsy already wasn't liking me so much, and now I was the reason she had to have her tonsils out. We had adjoining cribs with a glass with chicken wire inside it between us. Salem hospital put all little kids in cribs, but Patsy was seven and I was just turning six, and we were mortified to be in a crib. It didn't help when I saw Patsy smile as she watched me getting a shot in my bare bottom. Our tonsils came out and we went home to drink cold ice cream shakes, a real treat. The entire medical theory about tonsils being the enemy was reversed before I had my children. It seems the more current research demonstrates that they provide some immunity to disease.

After our operations, thank goodness, my mother told Patsy and me her story about having her tonsils removed. As she told it, the traveling doctor came around the homes to pull out children's tonsils when she was a child in the 1930s. On Old Linebrook Road in Ipswich, they would gather a bunch of kids and line them up in chairs in the kitchen. Without anesthesia, the doctor would go in with forceps and scalpel and cut out the tonsils, making a bloody mess that my mom saw close-up. She took off running! She told us many times that she almost got away! She told us this to remind us how lucky we were that we were asleep during our operation. I was just glad my breath didn't upset the teacher anymore!

On a little street named Pine Avenue, just off Haswell Park where I lived, resided a woman named Georgia Lewis. She was a second-grade teacher at the time at the Howe-Manning School. Mrs. Lewis did not yet have any children of her own. I think that is how I got so lucky! She came into my first-grade class a few times and seemed to take a special interest in me. She then made a proposal to my parents that saved my academic soul. Mrs. Lewis made a generous offer to tutor me in her home over the summer, for free! My mom didn't care, and I was very excited. I'm not so sure my father was happy, because we had lots of chores to get done every day in the summer before he returned home from work. My mother always started yelling, about mid-afternoon, "Stop playing and get your work done! Your father will be home in three hours, get that wood into the bulkhead." She yelled again at two hours and really yelled when we had only an hour left to finish it before he got home. When we had about forty-five minutes left, we worked furiously and always got it done. I knew I would have plenty of time to get the work done, even if I was at Mrs. Lewis's house half the day, and I wanted to learn to read.

It turned out to be only an hour or two that I got to learn to read at Mrs. Lewis's house, but it was five days a week. With one-on-one help all summer, I made progress quickly. The proverbial light bulb went on in my literacy-deprived farm brain. It made sense—it didn't sound like a moaning AAAAAA or growling RRRRRR anymore! As important to the learning was the fact that Mrs. Lewis believed I had potential— enough potential to invest her personal time and energy in me! She was a great teacher and seemed to like me. I was also impressed by her house. Not that it was extravagant; it was a Victorian-style small country home. It had something I had never seen in my own home: fresh lilacs or other cut flowers in vases on top of crocheted white dollies on every little mahogany table. It smelled wonderful!

That was the first time I realized some people lived differently than we did. I was welcomed into the home of an educated person and treated as a special guest at the young age of almost seven. I will always be indebted to Mrs. Lewis for her kindness. She didn't just tutor me; she made sure I didn't go back to the turtle reading group. Evidently, as I found out later, she had a difficult time convincing the principal that I could do the work. He adamantly believed that the background of a child's parents was the primary factor determining their future abilities in education. Mrs. Lewis would hear none of it. She persevered and staked her professional reputation on her belief that I could excel in her second-grade class in a high reading group. The principal reluctantly allowed it. Even at my young age and with my parents not actively supporting the move, I instinctively knew that this highly educated teacher believed I had the ability to succeed in her classroom, the classroom where reading was fluent, exciting, and made sense!

Although I was not a perfect teacher, as every good teacher is always striving to be better, this turning point early in my life was a lesson that helped me be better. I would never, as a teacher, presume that a child had little potential. I would rally for a parent and child when I sat at a meeting and witnessed a negative prediction, not one based on medical challenges, but one based on intelligence tests and judgment of the parent's education and income level. I would sometimes sit next to the parent and face the administrators, having empathy for the parent and ready to support him or her. Sometimes, I would disagree when the news was that their child did not have a disability, knowing they would not get the early intervention in kindergarten they would need to be successful. Other times, I would reassure the parent that one test, at one point in their child's short life, did not dictate their academic future. Just knowing a teacher believes in you can make all the difference in a child's life. It did for me!

The principal met with my parents to discuss my placement. I honestly don't know why he felt he had to. According to my mom, who told me often and consistently, the principal said that I was the only one of their children with some potential, that they shouldn't expect Patsy to get any special placements. All this was discussed in front of all of us children, leading me to be dubbed by my sisters, with both distain and sarcasm, "the smart one." My parents highly respected an educated man like the principal; they took his words as gospel. They were not upset but began to, without consciousness I believe, turn our lives into what was predicted. I got the first encyclopedia of every set in the grocery store to read; the letter A was always only forty-nine cents. My sisters got horses to ride!

⚘ ENGAGED AT SEVEN! ⚘

My confidence in school seemed to carry over a bit into my social life. Toward the end of second grade, large groups of children, including myself, had to walk to St. Agnes Church after school. Without adult supervision, at seven or eight years of age, we left the Howe-Manning School, crossed Route 114 in Middleton Square without any traffic light, traveled down 114, also known as South Main Street, to Route 62, also named Boston Street, and walked to the church. We were preparing for our First Communion. My mother really liked and respected Father Paul Donohue, as did the community. One classmate, Bobby Brown, walked close to me, and even held my hand once. There were a lot of distractions in addition to a cute boy holding my hand. Downtown Middleton had a post office, hardware store, and drugstore. There was also a small A&P grocery store, where we shopped with my mom and filled Green Stamps books to get free stuff. The grocery store closed up during my childhood; after that my mom went all the way to Peabody for groceries. She never went to Danvers unless it was to Almy's at the Danvers Plaza. The A&P was delightful. The aisles were very small and congested, the grocery carriages half the size that they are today. Frost's Hardware was an exciting place to be. Mrs. Frost was always nice to us kids. I remember enjoying the delicious sunflower seeds; she had a huge galvanized can of them and sold them by the pound. We could get a small bag for a few cents and did so for a few years until she saw me eat one on the way out the door. "You children aren't eating them yourselves, are you? Oh, my! Those are only for feeding birds. They may have mice droppings in them." She ruined a good thing but was very sweet about it!

Frost's Hardware had the absolute best wooden case with a locked glass front. It held BBs, caps, fishing hooks, and a big tray of the prettiest rings I had ever seen. Bobby picked out a diamond "engagement" ring from the foam holder and put it on my finger. I'd never had a boy spend any money on me, and here was Bobby, spending ten cents! I was the happiest seven-year-old walking to church that day!

☙ THE BOMB ❧

It was imminent! Be prepared! Children of the early fifties were raised on the constant fear of the "Bomb." The "Red Scare," the anti-communist hysteria, put us in fear of a Soviet nuclear attack. Thank goodness we all felt confident that, if we just followed the advice of the American government, we would emerge from our bomb shelters or out from under our desks at school just fine! The air-raid drills stopped just before I entered first grade, but we still knew to "duck and cover," as my older sister was taught. When we built our little ranch home, a special room was made in the basement. It was the bomb shelter. In it would go the best of my mom's home canned foods, including homemade root beer, pickles, jams, and vegetables. We would survive on some delicious foods.

In 1951, the Civil Defense Administration prepared many materials to instruct and calm the public. The people had trust in the government and followed rules well. The effects generating from a 10-megaton atomic bomb were downplayed, with little mention of radiation sickness. The official Civil Defense hat was given to all schoolteachers, who were tasked with leading their students to safety in the hall or under their desks in case of an attack. The administration would also send you, on request, precise instructions on how to build the best bomb shelter. It said to use thick stones so more radiation would be deflected and the safer you would be. People were not to come out of their shelters until they hear the "all clear" siren. A somber fact was that New York City, in 1953, issued 2.5 million free dog tags to students in public, private, and parochial schools. Yet we still felt competent and not afraid.

Bert the Turtle made us feel safer. We were encouraged to just sing along to his "Duck and Cover" song in the Civil Defense public cartoon. The narrator gave us a few scenarios. "Here's Tony going to his Cub Scout meeting. Tony knows a bomb could explode any time of the year, day or night. There's a bomb! Duck! And cover!" *Life* was a trustworthy and popular magazine. It stated that ninety-seven out of one hundred people would survive an attack if they were in a bomb shelter. Now, everybody knew that!

Actively participating in your own survival gives people a sense of empowerment. There was still trust in the government in the early fifties. Blind optimism is not always a bad thing when the alternative was too horrendous to consider.

☙ RED RUBBER BOOTS ❧

I was so proud of my brand-new red rubber boots. I was in the first grade and I'd had a tough school year so far, but spring might be better! Nobody else had ever worn them, not even my older sister. They didn't come cheap, but the cost was only the beginning of the quest to attain a new pair of boots. Mom and I took a trip down Route 114 all the way to Peabody and its exciting new Northshore Mall. J.J. Newbury's had shoes on the lower floor and a scary escalator took you down to them. I held tight onto my mom's coat. It was such a treat to have a shopping trip with just her, a rare early evening that my dad stayed home with the other kids. I'm thinking that our good friends Bob and Louise—we only knew them as a couple—were also at our house watching my sisters.

After trying on several pair, being helped by a young man working the shoe department, and feeling totally entitled, I decided on a bright red rubber rain boot. They were about eight inches high with one button. To tighten them you just folded the top sideways and attached the rubber to the button with an elastic cord. I was in love with those boots! The salesman noticed my delight and said I could wear them home. The boots were made to fit right over your shoes back then. As we stepped onto the escalator to go up to the main floor, I beamed! I turned my feet sideways as if I were wearing Cinderella's slippers! We ascended and at the top, just before I could step off, the top of one of the boots was grabbed under the end plate. I screamed as the toe of my new boot started to turn into ground red rubber. My mother looked back, grabbed me, and jerked me free of the escalator's grip. The store manager and a crowd of shoppers stared at us. I cried so hard I'm sure they thought my toes were ripped off by the escalator. I thought it couldn't have been any worse. The boots were destroyed, but the manager promised us new ones, and he had the shoe salesman bring up an identical pair. He made sure all the gawking customers heard him promise us a new pair, saying several times, "She is fine, just the boots were hurt." I quickly recovered, although I must admit I don't like escalators very much, even as an adult.

The next day, I proudly wore my new red boots to school, putting them under my jacket in the huge closet area that was covered when the blackboard came down in front of it. At dismissal, when I went to get my coat and boots, the boots were gone. Only a few kids had been dismissed before me, and the teacher must have noticed the boots walking out the door. She wrote a note to my mom explaining that another girl had taken my boots. She put the girl's name in the note, also. My mother was furious! Weeks of saved-up dollars from grocery money went to pay for those boots. She said, "Get in the car," and I did! We pulled up in front of an old farmhouse and she grabbed my hand and dragged me up to the door with her. A man came out before we even knocked and without my even knowing him, he scared me. Standing up as straight as I have ever seen her, and with a sharp voice, my mom said, "Your daughter stole my girl's brand-new boots, and I want them back now!" He turned and went back into the house, coming out a few minutes later with the boots. Without a word, Mom took them. We walked back to the car and went home. I just kept staring at Mom, both proud and amazed. I clutched those boots firmly in my lap with a huge smile on my face.

Later that night, I heard my mom telling my father the story. Evidently, the family was even poorer than we were. The old farmhouse was extremely rundown. It seems the children were known to be unruly. The kids in this family put on a very tough front, most likely a survival instinct. The father was also known to be very domineering and strict, a strong taskmaster to his kids. My father was not too happy that Mom had stormed over there with just me by her side. Mom's inner lioness never came out with my father, but I had seen it twice now. She had stood up to bullies for me, both this man and my uncle!

⚡ FIRE! ⚡

Although my dad was a very strong man, both physically and emotionally, he did have an area that caused him anguish and worry. That was fire. The extravagant fire alarm system he insisted on in the new house was one example. Another was his reaction to an incident a few years later. The twins, Jeanne and Janet, were trying to get a campfire going on the ice of our swamp. The older kids from the farm did this often, but at only seven or eight years old, the twins couldn't carry the can of gas easily. As they often did when trying to carry heavy things, they worked together with a broomstick through the handle. Unlike other things they carried this way, the smooth handle allowed the gas can to slide back and forth as they walked. The gas can did not have a cover and it was a long way to the pond, with gas splashing on them. After finally getting to the pond, as they tried to pour the gas on the wood, more gas splashed on their clothes. My father came upon them just as they were striking matches to light the fire. He first smelled, and then saw the gas on their clothes and the matches in their hands. Jeanne and Janet said he moved so fast he shocked them. Grabbing one child, and most certainly in panic mode, he started spanking the first one he caught, the other twin saw that and ran for it, hiding where she could still see. After looking for the other one and not being able to tell them apart, he grabbed the same twin again and spanked her, thinking it was the other! He didn't calm down until two spankings had been given.

Later, when he finally calmed down, he told my mom that they would have burned to death if he hadn't caught them trying to light the fire. For years, Jeanne and Janet bickered in a joking manner about the day one got two beatings and the other got none! My mother was just amazed that, although twins, their own father still couldn't tell them apart.

❧ OUR PET TURTLES ❧

Little green turtles: they were so cute. They came from the pet store and never grew much bigger than a half dollar. The cage had some water and rocks and a few little pretend trees. It wasn't as if they could do tricks or anything, but we enjoyed our little pets. Then the newspaper announced that these non-native green turtles could carry salmonella and make children sick. Mom had a great idea.

"They will be so happy living in the swamp. You play in there all the time so you will still see them. Go let them free!"

The water was very low that year. We were pumping from the one deep hole for the garden, and it hadn't rained much lately. There was over twelve feet between the dry edge of the swamp and the beginning of the dark black water. In between was mud. My sisters and I said some words of goodbye before we gently placed the turtles at the edge of the mud. They instinctively knew to head for the water, so we cheered them on as they pumped their little legs into the mud, moving forward slowly. Our cheering stopped when we saw the large heads of several of the huge black snakes that lived in the swamp. They were emerging at the edge of the water. Before we could think to get a big stick, the snakes had slithered forward into the mud. They each swallowed a turtle. We could see our pet turtles' legs still moving just inside the mouths of the snakes and we couldn't do a thing to save them. We screamed, we cried, we threw little sticks at those snakes. The moving bulge of our little pet turtles moved back from the snake's mouth and we knew there was no saving them. Slowly they slid back into the black water, black on black, invisible to our eyes. We walked back to the house, still crying, still in shock. Mom was doing laundry in the cellar and we entered from the cellar door. She didn't look our way before saying, "Now aren't those turtles much happier in the swamp?"

ELEMENTARY SCHOOL TEACHERS,
⚘ GRADES THREE TO SIX ⚘

My grades were good, but the most memorable thing about the rest of elementary school was the quirky teachers. After Mrs. Lewis, I have little recollection of my third- and fourth-grade teachers. My report card listed my third-grade teacher as Mrs. Nanis and my fourth-grade teacher as Mrs. Abend. In third grade, Mrs. Nanis wrote in the first quarter comments section: "Sandra's work is good, but can be improved with practice in handwriting." In the second quarter, Mrs. Nanis wrote, "Sandra's spelling has improved but she still needs drill on arithmetic facts." My mom then wrote, in nice cursive, "I've helped her with spelling and now I will drill her on number facts." I am thankful my mom replied and assume she helped me, but I don't remember being helped at home. My mom had her hands full with so much work caring for my grandmother. I did jump from grade level academics to a grade higher by the final quarter, so I must have worked harder. Just a note, memorization of number facts has never been a strength for me, and made all future math courses very challenging.

In fourth grade, I got all Bs in both scholarship and effort, and no comments were written for any quarter, so it must have been a mediocre year in most ways! I am sure my mom was happy the teacher didn't ask her to help me anymore. I did miss five days in the third quarter. I must have had some illness, as most all my school years after first grade I had almost perfect attendance. Fifth grade was memorable because of one teacher. She stays in the minds of many, for better or for worse. Depending on how much she liked you, your experience would be totally different, mostly for the boys. One young man, obviously having committed some infraction, saw a spanking coming from her and put his hand over his bottom. Unfortunately for her, he still had his pencil in his hand with the point facing out. It almost went through her hand when she spanked him. She needed to see the nurse, and that boy was in even bigger trouble, although nobody in class thought he deliberately held the pencil that way. It was an instinctive defensive move! Even so, I'm sure he got a real beating at home, because most of our parents felt that the teacher was always right, even if they were wrong. This teacher was a "larger and lovelier" woman who wore so much perfume that I couldn't get anywhere near her without almost being sick. She must have thought me very emotional as I always had teary eyes in her presence. I still have allergies, with zero tolerance for expensive perfumes, making church services impossible for me. During a parent-teacher conference thirty years later, the parent asked me why I always had tears running down my face when speaking so highly of her son. Apparently, she felt I may have had conflicting feelings. I reassured her that it had nothing to do with her son and everything to do with her perfume! Gimmie-Sue explained that she wore only the most expensive perfume. I politely told her that women's expensive and all men's smelly products were the scents I had the most allergic reactions to!

In her early years she would have the boys take turns giving her back rubs throughout the day, something obviously not appropriate by today's standards of conduct for teachers. I do believe she was asked not to do this in the years after I was in her class, but my husband remembers it well. Many days she would bring her very artistic teenaged son into class, and he would entertain us with his cartoon drawings.

Mr. Winter, functioning as a sixth-grade teacher at the time, was an incredible man, but not a very effective teacher during the year I was in sixth grade. He couldn't be. Many of the boys that year were so incorrigible that it was almost impossible to teach. Mr. Winter was so nice, they walked all over him. Many of the boys had stayed back, some more than once. It was more like a high school that year, with boys growing beards, changing voices, and starting fights. Many had severe reading problems, but dyslexia and other reading disabilities had not yet been studied thoroughly, and the general consensus was that they were just lazy kids. That year was a good example illustrating why retention is usually not such a good idea. Academic difficulties without any remediation, combined with raging male hormones, is not a recipe for success in a classroom. Mr. Winter never lost it, always remaining a gentle person, but the other pupils didn't learn very much in class. As a teacher he tried to find ways for the challenged learners as well as the higher achievers to find a niche. He became a good mentor for the boys he picked to be audiovisual helpers and patrol officers. In a one-on-one situation, he really inspired many kids to take an interest in things other than just fighting. Mr. Winter found his own niche later in life and was brilliant with archeological research.

My best friend, Cheryl Bowes, and I stuck together and stayed fairly innocent. We loved playing "ball against the wall" games on the brick walls near the cafeteria back door. Chanting and bouncing, clapping and swinging our legs over the small rubber ball, we stayed entertained and out of the way of the more mature kids. We also had little toy animals that would walk down our desktops when we lifted the top to a slight incline. This was probably more like fourth or fifth grade, as they were really cute! I wish I could have stayed innocent, and I would have if I'd spent all my time at the Bowes household! On my sixth-grade report card, Cheryl wrote, "Good Bye, Cheryl Bowes." We both knew, heading to a huge three-town junior high and high school, our days of simple childhood play were over. One of my sixth-grade teachers wrote, "Sandy—Many successes to a sweet, hard working girl, JM Foley." Miss Ruark, another sixth-grade teacher, wrote, "Best Wishes" with her signature. My grades were all As in reading categories, as I was reading above seventh-grade level. My penmanship went from a B minus to a solid B!

I feel I need to mention that one entire side of our report cards was devoted to "Health and Safety Habits, Social Habits, and Work Habits." I always got checkmarks in the "Almost Always" box. I find it interesting that, as a child who never wanted to break the rules and upset my parents, I got a check-plus in grade three in the section "Respects rights and opinions of others." The same teacher, Mrs. Nanis, among all the checks put only a dot in the "cleanliness" section; it was in the "almost always" box, but I think she had some ambiguity about that decision. That once-a-week bath and everyday farm work didn't always leave us Blais kids fresh as daises by mid-week!

⚘ HASWELL PARK ⚘

The street we lived on was a mixture of old and new families, camps and new homes. It began as summer camps for the city folk from Lynn, Peabody, and even East Boston to escape to for the summer. As people began to relocate permanently to our little town, most camps were renovated, but some were demolished, and ranch or small cape homes replaced them. The street was paved and had streetlights as well as town water lines. Everybody knew each other. Children played in the street, as people drove slowly and carefully. The elementary school bus came as far as the last loop, out of sight of our house. The high school bus did not come down the road; the teens walked to Route 114 to catch the bus. Groups of kids played together without any adult supervision. As pre-teens, we found hide-and-seek at dusk always exciting. A sweet and shy boy, Mikey, actually stole a kiss on my cheek as we hid together on the inside steps of his bulkhead. When it got dark, and the streetlights came on, we ran home. I was probably still blushing from my first kiss!

We didn't sleep over at friends' houses on the street. They didn't make any kind of nighttime Pull-Ups for kids that wet the bed; I'm sure that factor also played into decisions not to do overnights anywhere. I don't recall any other kids going to sleepovers either. We only stayed over a few nights on our visits to my Uncle Eddie's camp on Crystal Lake in New Hampshire, and that was after my younger sisters were ten years old or so. Jeanne and Janet also had a weeklong camping trip, a freebie from a church group and run by nuns in New Hampshire. I didn't pay much attention, but I remember they told my mom to never make them do that again! Jeanne and Janet spent more time with my younger cousin, Denise, on the farm next door, and were getting more interested in owning a horse. Their dream would soon come true.

My dad was a homebody, and money was very tight. For most of our growing-up years, my mother did in-house nursing care for our grandmother. It would have been hard to get somebody to stay overnight. Even after Mémère, my father's mother, passed on, my parents never took vacations without us kids, although I'm sure my mom would have loved one. I never heard her ask my father to go away as a couple. On our day excursions, my father would always say to all of us, "I wonder what the poor people are doing?" He felt these little trips were a bit of extravagance, and he was right! We felt very lucky!

❧ PARENTS DON'T PLAY! ❧

During the fifties and early sixties, at least among the families and kids I played with, children entertained themselves. There was no expectation that a parent would play with you. Even though I was hyper aware that my mom did not have a moment to spare for frivolous play, even other moms in the neighborhood who had much fewer demands on their time did not play with their children. I never once saw a mom or dad playing with kids on our street. In fact, I think it would have been considered weird!

There were Brownies and Girl Scouts as well as Boy Scouts, and this was the "proper" place for adult-child interactions. Church groups were also a place for adults with time on their hands and an interest in children to actively volunteer. I believe Patsy and I did Girl Scouts for a short while. I know I did, as I was very proud of the badges I earned, although Kate Bailey probably had the most badges of any Girl Scout in town. Mrs. Martinuk taught my troop, which met at the SMIA (South Middleton Improvement Association) hall on River Street. During one of the last meetings I attended, a huge paper wasp nest came flying in through the window, fully loaded with wasps. It seems Kate's sister, Martha, didn't want to be a Girl Scout; she was expressing her opinion of the entire organization with her act of terror! Her mother gave up sending her to Girl Scouts, and girls were not allowed in Boy Scouts, so Martha stuck with sports. Most of the town appreciated Martha's tremendous abilities in baseball. As young mothers in the nineties, Martha and I developed a great friendship that has sustained the test of time. We both loved adventures with our children—goofy, crazy, fun adventures. As senior citizens, we still have adventures that make us laugh, and sometimes embarrass our husbands!

Children were not enrolled in abundant activities as they often are today. A "scheduled" activity for us would take place exactly when the wild blueberries were ready for picking. That was the closest thing to quality time that we had with my mom, as it got all of us out of the house and into nature together. She must have arranged for somebody to watch Nana and then Mémère over the years, because they could never be left alone. Blueberries were an acceptable excuse for an escape! There was nothing as great as a day in the woods with Mom near our house in the warm summer sun. Without cell phones, which hadn't been invented yet, we were out of reach, and all the tasks of caregiving or just working to survive were forgotten. Light chatter mixed with total silence made for an enjoyable day. Aunt Opal was the absolute top picker out of all of us, and my mother admired her greatly. I often tripped and spilled half my berries walking through the bushes on the way home. The ones I had left I would cherish. We had a cast-iron handled "pie maker," a device that held two pieces of buttered bread, blueberries, and a bit of sugar. You'd clamp it shut, cut off the edges of the bread sticking out, and put it over the flame of the gas stove. The "toasted pie" was delicious! The best part is that we made these all by ourselves anytime we wanted to, as long as we used our own blueberries. This cast-iron pie maker has been a coveted item in my family for generations now. What amazed us was my mom's generosity. We could not believe that she would use up all her blueberries in one regular-size pie that she would then share with company! She really was a saint.

Even during major building projects, such as the three-story treehouse my sisters and I constructed in a cluster of trees near the house, there was no adult participation or support. My father's main concern was how many of his ten-penny spike nails we used! My mom or dad never went up into our fort, and that is just how we liked it. In the winter, we often built snow sculptures and snow forts right in the front yard, so mom never had to worry. She did worry about us catching cold, and insisted that we wear heavy coats and wool mittens. It was good that we had hot water radiators to dry our wet clothes on. The smell of steaming wet wool permeated the house after an afternoon playing in the snow.

In our house, the children did not ever have a say in what television shows were watched on the one television. We were lucky that our dad loved the *Three Stooges*. Our house was small enough that when sitting at the small island in the kitchen, you could see and hear the television in the living room. Only mom and dad sat at the island; we either sat at the dining room table between the two rooms or the couch in the living room. It usually depended on how slippery the food was on our plates. If we sat in the dining room, we had to space out so mom and dad could see the television between us. For years we shared our supper with Moe, Larry, and Curly. This was our time to laugh, although I am sure it never added to any cultural or spiritual growth within us!

Mom and Dad both enjoyed *Professional Wrestling*, which I constantly told them was fake! After many years of hearing the screams from my mom—"he's got a razor, watch out," and, "Oh no, he grabbed a metal chair and hit him over the head"—I stopped making any commentaries. Even though he played the villain role when wrestling, Killer Kowalski, a Polish immigrant from Ontario, Canada, was their favorite wrestler. The World Wide Wrestling Foundation put on exciting matches, televised in homes all over our area. The former boxing champion, Jack Dempsey, was a guest referee one night, and was seriously hurt, so I had to admit that it wasn't always fake. In the sixties, they started tag-team matches, adding more screams from my mom as she watched. After I graduated high school, my parents started to talk more about Andre the Giant, but then, Killer Kowalski pinned even him. Later, they were able to afford tickets to see a live professional wrestling match in a nearby city. I was still living at home while attending college and I saw two forlorn people return home that night. They told me it was really fake! They stopped watching televised wrestling, but still always spoke fondly of Killer Kowalski. Kowalski retired and started a wrestling school about twenty miles away in Malden, Massachusetts. By the time I was an older teen in college, they started going to the Fine Arts movie theater in Beverly, well known for its risqué films. After they'd complained about my late nights writing on my manual typewriter, I'd moved my bedroom down to the cellar, which was not nice but very private. But my sisters recall hearing weird noises coming from my parents' bedroom on those movie nights. Although they were finally enjoying some affection, at that time I thought it was just too gross to even think about!

Even though my parents never had much time for interactions, we had a few fun outings with them every year. A drive to the White Mountains of New Hampshire was a really big deal. In the winter, we went to see cars racing on the ice of Lake Winnipesaukee. In the summer, we saw the Man in the Mountain profile in the rocks of Franconia Notch and walked the Flume. We could get comfortable in the back seat of the car as there were no seat belts or car seat requirements. Sometimes one of us would wedge up into the rear view window to ride. There was a cord across the top of the back seat to hold on to if my father turned a corner too fast. We always carried extra water in case the engine overheated. We rarely, if ever, had drinks or ate food in the car while driving. As a family with small bladders, that would require too many bathroom stops! I also don't remember drive-through food establishments on every corner; in fact, I don't think there were any in the country. There were ice cream drive-ups, though. The most famous, Richardson's Dairy, was only a short walk from our home.

❧ PING PONG ❧

My father and I shared one common interest during my younger adolescent years: ping pong. My dad had played when in the Army during the Korean conflict and was very skilled. He was fast and agile. All of us four kids had turns playing. But only I kept at it and became good enough of a challenge to keep Dad interested. It was such a joy to have Dad all to myself. The ping pong table was set up in the cellar among all his woodworking tools. The exposed rafters of the house, the huge shelves of supplies, and the piles of wood all made retrieving a wayward ping pong ball a challenge. This made it frustrating to play with anyone not aligned in skills, as far too much time was spent looking for the ball. Finally, it was just him and I. We played for hours on many evenings. He would "put some French" on the ball, as he said, making it spin and harder to return, but I got better and better. I remember very clearly the night I actually beat my father at the game. He didn't act mad or disappointed, but shortly after that he said he had to make room for more woodworking projects and the table was put away. I believe he was proud that he had taught me so well, but I do have those rose-colored glasses and want to believe what he never did verbalize. I will always treasure the gift of quality time we spent together.

☀ THE BLAIS FARM AFTER WE MOVED ☀

Although we lived in a different house, we still spent a lot of time on the Blais farm. I was particularly close to my cousin Roger, as we were the same age. Roger, being the first boy in his family, was worked very hard by his father; we rarely had time for play. I was doing very well in school and getting to the library often enough to immerse myself in stories, an escape of a sort for me. For my cousins, the only way to escape was to hide out. Roger and I had our favorite spot way down in one of the cow pastures. We had pushed an old chair up against the back of a big tree facing away from the barns and garage. We would sit and talk, both squished together in the big chair. Sometimes I helped with the chores, but only if my uncle was not around, as I was very afraid of him. I loved feeding the cows from the horse trailer full of Hostess products that my uncle picked up at the thrift bread store. He pulled the old horse trailer to the back of the thrift store and packed it high, then parked it inside the cow pasture. We would sit inside the trailer on top of the huge pile of "old" goodies. Each item had to be unwrapped before throwing it to the cows, as cows should not eat paper. It was a tedious task made much better by the fact that nothing was really that old and we never had snacks like this at home. Besides, we reasoned, the cows didn't like marshmallow covering over chocolate cake with cream in the middle, also branded as SnoBalls. The expiration date might have been long past, but these processed foods had so many preservatives in them they didn't mold or taste bad, in fact, the Twinkies, Ding Dongs, and cupcakes tasted very good! We would sit and unwrap and laugh and life was good.

I tried to stay away from the barn when looking for Roger, although sometimes I would have to go in there to find him. My cousin Joanie always squirted me with hot milk from the cow's teat and I couldn't stand that! She always seemed to be milking a cow. Roger would bring me into the kitchen when his mom was off working at her jobs off the farm. He often made what he usually made for his own lunch and was called a "concoction." I didn't drink more than a sip of his eggs, milk, and fruit blend as my mom had told us our stomach was not used to unpasteurized milk. Plus, I don't like crunching on eggshells.

After we moved into our small house, the big Blais farmhouse was usually freezing. Without my father to keep the wood boiler going, my uncle's family relied on the huge fireplace in the kitchen of the big drafty house. The house was often full of smoke, and my cousin's clothes always smelled of a wood fire. When they had cut firewood, no visitor was allowed in the house without carrying in an armful of it. My uncle, Frenchy, or later called Hitler, would yell to every visitor to bring in a handful of firewood. Many townsfolk who stopped by the farm talked of the long logs that would stick out of the living room window. After running out of cut firewood, my uncle would have the kids push a tree, with the limbs trimmed off, through the window into the fireplace. They would just push it farther into the fire as it burned. My father and many observers would just shake their heads, as much heat was lost out the window. One time it was so cold that one of the younger boys pulled his entire bed up to the large open fireplace, seeking its warmth. In the middle of the night, his mattress caught fire. His siblings and father just rolled the mattress into the fireplace and let it burn. My Aunt Opal was working the eleven to seven shift at the state hospital, which she did for many years. She must have wondered why they were short one mattress when she got home the next morning!

Another event that happened that some find hard to believe, although we witnessed it: One daughter was lucky enough to have the largest bedroom at the far end of the house downstairs, but unluckily enough that her radiators froze and burst. The system kept pumping water, which covered her entire bedroom floor before finally stopping; without heat in the basement under her room, it quickly froze. Several of the kids put on ice skates and actually skated on her floor!

Most of the older Blais kids had been given or bought electric blankets; I believe that is one reason they would not get out of bed to go to school in the winter. My father would sit and wait in our driveway as one or two would come running to catch a ride to St. Joseph's in Salem, but often he had to leave without any passengers. After years of this, my uncle finally let the kids go to Middleton public schools. I can't imagine being cold all the time, but, nonetheless, I believe the cold temperatures of the house helped my cousins stay so healthy. We, on the other hand, had to wear bulky wool coats if my mother even felt a small chill. Our house was about eighty degrees with red-hot radiators. We were sick more often than any of my cousins.

The boiler in our house kept the radiators hot, and because it also made hot water for laundry and bathing, we were often overheated. My dad got all the reject wooden game parts from Parker Brothers, and they burned more like coal. Wooden Monopoly houses, dominoes, and even Ouija boards in large drums were his for the taking. We always joked that the only accurate thing the Ouija board predicted was that we would be really warm! My mom once stored all her bottles of homemade root beer on their sides under the radiator in the enclosed porch room, not expecting the radiator to come on in the summer. Evidently somebody needed a bath, the radiator got hot, and about fifty bottles of root beer exploded and frothed the entire floor in sticky soda!

We still enjoyed playing on the Blais farm. This great climbing tree was in the front cow pasture.

⚡ EARLY FUN ⚡

A night out for the family was seeing a movie at the Middleton Drive-in. We'd bring homemade popcorn in a huge brown paper bag with butter staining the entire outside—a huge treat during the movie. Mom also packed drinks, usually a big pitcher of Kool-Aid or ZaRex. For a dollar, it was a really fun night. The speaker hung on the driver's side window and my father never forgot to disconnect it before driving off. As we went to the drive-in only on warm Saturday nights a few times each summer, it was special! Saturday was always a full day of work for us, cutting and hauling wood with my dad. At the drive-in, the one thing we all had to take turns doing was scratching my dad's head over the back of the seat, while sawdust flew out of his hair. After that, Mom would sit closer to him! The movie *Old Yeller* made me cry for days. I was only five or six, and it took me a long time to get over that dog having to be killed. I also have never felt comfortable talking or thinking about wild boars. One of the last movies we saw together as a family was *Son of Flubber*. I was about eleven and was ready to start going to the drive-in with my friends. Before having cars, the young teens sat on the high rocks up behind the kid's playground. You didn't pay when you came through the back from the fields, but you also didn't have any soundtrack for the movie. This was where many kids tried their first cigarette. I did, and I felt really sick and never smoked again. The drive-in was the best motivator for getting a car! We sat up there with envy, thinking how much fun those older kids were having in their cars. We could only imagine as so many windows were fogged up.

Visiting Uncle Eddie and Aunt Doe was always a good time. In the summer, visiting them at the camp they rented on Crystal Lake in New Hampshire was the best. This was when Uncle Eddie was his most relaxed and sociable; he seemed a bit gruff much of the time when we visited him at home. They had a nice boat, and Dana and Nancy were avid water skiers. My cousin Dana was my age, and his sister Nancy was a few years older. Nancy was always so sophisticated and glamorous. She had beautiful dark hair and was pretty, very smart, and mature. Nancy was a role model for me; I wanted to be just like her. I wanted to have "class," but if I acted classy my parents accused me of thinking I was better than they were. It was hard when I couldn't even call the evening meal "dinner" without being accused of trying to be somebody I wasn't.

Being on a lake made us kids aware that our father had never learned how to swim. It's unfathomable that a kid growing up on the ocean in Danvers, near the Salem border, never learned to swim. I suppose he was too busy helping his dad run a horse and buggy service from Danvers to Salem. But he wasn't afraid of the water! He would put on three life preservers, belts that strapped around your waist, before he would swing out over the lake on the rope swing, crashing into water that was way over his head. He did it once without the life belts, looking like Tarzan with his muscled and wiry body. He popped to the top with a smile on his face and kicked his way in. These rare moments I cherish the most—Dad having fun.

A very talented man who lived across town on Liberty Street, a Frenchman named Mr. Levesque, built sulkies for race horses. Once he made a water ski seat on a whim. My father borrowed it from him and we took it to the lake. Uncle Eddie had Nancy driving the boat, several spotters in the stern, and my mom on shore with binoculars. They all watched my father settle himself on the seat, which was supported by wide, wooden skis and connected to the boat via a pull rope attached to the front between the skis. Uncle Eddie had Nancy gunning the engine, but it was a heavy load. Although my father was a small man and weighed little ,even with three life preservers strapped on him, the wooden skis and seat were heavy. Eventually he was on top of the wake and riding high, but it didn't last long. The curve on the front of one ski caught under the wake but dad held on, until the other ski went under and the entire thing headed down, along with my father, who hung on tightly. My mom screamed from shore, "He is down, he is down." Eddie figured more speed was needed, so had Nancy push it to the max. The rope stayed taught, but it seemed my dad was traveling under instead of on top of the lake. Finally, we saw the top of the skis. Dad was still hanging on, and he was on top of the wake, but it looked like the seat was going down again. Uncle Eddie stopped the boat. My mom was shaken up, but all my father had to say was, "I knew it had to come up again sooner or later and I was coming up with it."

My mom was deathly afraid of water. She loved the beach, but several times she panicked and thought she was drowning in two feet of water. Because she wanted us to learn to swim, and neither she nor my dad knew how, they sent us to the Danvers YMCA, where the town for a short time offered lessons in between using Thunder Bridge and Paradise Park for that purpose. I was so scared at the YMCA—not of the water, but the strange environment. I didn't like having lots of kids kicking and splashing me. I didn't like changing in the bathrooms. I didn't like the chorine smell. I finally finished the session, graduating as a "polliwog," the least skilled swimming category they offered. I eventually taught myself to swim and was able to swim at the lake, although never very gracefully or efficiently. I did try water skiing and did okay on two skis. My cousins were dropping a ski and doing tricks, but then again, they spent most of the summer on the lake!

I just love how free and easy summer seemed to be when drifting on an old wooden rowboat on the lake. Dana had restored it enough to make it hold about five of us! My cousin and I were never very close, but I felt included and comfortable on the lake with his other cousins and friends. It was such an escape for my entire family; I am so appreciative that my aunt and uncle invited us. We went up only once or twice each summer, staying overnight only once that I remember, but I got to see my parents as a couple and having fun. It was a rare gift!

A rare and wonderful time was had at my Uncle Eddie's camp on Crystal Lake in New Hampshire. To see my parents laugh and relax was a gift. I will always be thankful for Uncle Eddie and Aunt Doe for the invites.

⚜ MY MOM'S BROTHER EDDIE HAS A FLASHBACK ⚜

It was tougher being the boy. My sister Ruthie did her share of cleaning the hundreds of rabbit cages, but the rest of the work fell to me. Ruthie might get locked in the basement with me by Mom, but she didn't get beaten by our father. Henry, my dad, seemed to feel Ruthie, being a girl, never deserved a beating! He even had an affectionate name for her, "Dot." I supposed she really didn't need to be disciplined, because she was too afraid to ever do anything wrong, but it still made me mad.

I had my pet goat, and all was good when my goat and I worked together. He mostly just followed me, and often made even more work, but I loved him. I could hug my goat and those were the only hugs I would ever know, unless I had to catch Ruthie from falling, and that wasn't really a hug because she was my sister and I had to catch her. Being tenant farmers in the Ipswich countryside was a lot of work. Sometimes I wished we were back in Somerville, in the city where my father was a butcher in a meat market. I know my mom, Katherine, liked it much better in the city; she really was miserable out here in the country. For me, finally having a pet of my own made it so much better. The crops paid off our tenancy and were important. The money from the rabbit meat and fur paid for our food and clothes. I really hated leaving my goat behind when I went to school, but he was always waiting for me in the yard when I returned. We would have a few moments of fun frolicking before Mom would yell to us to get to our chores. Ruthie really found cleaning hundreds of rabbit cages disgusting and didn't like that most of our meat meals were rabbit. As long as it was never goat I was happy!

It was fall and the gardens were packed with enormous amounts of tomatoes, squash, and many other vegetables. It would be a good year as tenant farmers. We sat down to supper together and I thought that farm life wasn't so bad after all. My father was very quiet, but that was usual for him. The only remark he made was that my pet goat had gotten into the garden while I was at school and eaten some vegetables. We finished eating but I was beginning to get a strange feeling in my belly, my supper wasn't sitting so well. My dad said to meet him outside and to bring along the goat, my best friend in life. I had to lead him to my father as my goat seemed to also sense my tension.

In a split second after arriving in the front yard, my dad took a ball peen hammer from his overall loop and smashed my goat right between the eyes, caving in his skull and squirting blood everywhere. His only words were, "That garden is our rent for this place." I was still clutching the rope in my hands, but my goat was a crumpled mess on the ground, his head bashed in and just a few death twitches still coming from his body. I didn't cry in front of my father; I think I was in shock. I loaded him in the wheelbarrow and lugged him way out beyond the vegetable fields. I did cry then, alone with my best friend, pushing my head into the only fur that wasn't bloodied. One last soft and still warm hug. Then I dug a hole and buried him; I was afraid my father would butcher him, and nobody was going to eat my pet goat for supper! I walked home pushing the empty wheelbarrow and nobody even tried to meet my stare. It would be a long time before I ever cried again. I don't think I ever called Henry "Dad" again.

⚜ HARSH REALITIES! ⚜

My parents wanted Patsy to take an interest in something; my mom wasn't too happy that it was rabbits. We didn't have rabbits, and mom had shared her angry stories about having to clean hundreds of cages as a child. Maybe that is why Patsy picked rabbits. She wanted to join Mr. Scott's Great Rabbit Club! My mom gave in and for a few weeks Patsy enjoyed the classes: how to care for rabbits and how to show them in 4H shows. One night when my mom picked her up from the class, she wouldn't talk and said she was never going back. When my mom asked Mr. Scott about it later, he said she didn't handle class very well that night. It was on how to butcher rabbits for meat!

When I overheard my parents talking, it reminded me of the one time we raised chickens as food. Not for eggs, but for meat! On killing day, we were supposed to help my father. When he cut off the heads, with us having to take turns holding the birds, a few of them flew up into a tree in our back yard. Patsy and I just stared in horror at a few headless chickens in a tree, and watched them quickly fall to the ground. I was both amazed and horrified; I just didn't understand how they could even know where to fly without a head. Patsy refused to eat chicken for that entire year. I can imagine that the "surprise" lesson on butchering rabbit for meat brought back all the chicken memories for her. And maybe a few more horrid visuals.

We had almost as many kittens in our little ranch house as we did on the farm. We had the cutest set of cuddly kittens and we kept them in the playhouse with a heavy pallet as a gate. A sudden big gust of wind pushed the heavy pallet in and crushed several of them. It was horrible; Mom had to bury the bodies of a few of our kittens. We felt so guilty for not securing the pallet more strongly. Another time we had pet ducks in a pen by the "swamp." Raccoons broke into their pen one night and decapitated most of them; however, two survived. They seemed okay until I was petting them about a week afterward. I brought them to Mom and told her it felt like there was a hole under the feathers on their back. She got her cure-all, a bottle of peroxide, and poured it under the feathers on their back. Right away, maggots started floating out of our ducks' backs. They returned to swim happily in the pond until they were eaten by huge snapping turtles. That's what we believe ate them, because we remembered the lesson very well that dad had taught us years before. A humongous snapper was on the dirt road to the pits, and Dad told us to watch what would happen to us if we went near it. He then proceeded to push a stick near the turtle's face, and it snapped the stick in half so fast our heads spun!

I don't think that being exposed to harsh realities of farm life or natural prey/predator events in nature are necessarily harmful. I do believe that not addressing them, not talking about them with your children, can have emotional implications that can stay with a child. My older sister did not talk about the intense feelings she had in reaction to chicken killing day. She kept it all inside. I verbalized everything! I also know my parents would never have tolerated any form of abuse for our pets. I am sure my mom was unaware our pet turtles would be eaten by snakes. In my family, we loved our pets!

⚶ CANNING ALL SUMMER ⚶

The garden was bursting with vegetables! Still, Mom would buy bushels of tomatoes from the local farms, the cheaper ones, especially for canning. Getting all her supplies out—huge water bath pot, gigantic pressure cooker, lids, bands, jar lifter, and more—was a monumental task, but the supplies stayed out all summer into fall. I observed every detail and helped whenever I could. The tomatoes ripened on the dining room table and we canned as they softened: boiling water plunge, skins taken off, and the pot full. My mom was very frugal, so she didn't even cook them down to sauce, just tomatoes in hundreds of jars to be used for many different recipes all winter. Just a teaspoon of salt, and nothing else! It should be said that we never had air conditioning in our home, just as I never did as a mom, so we canned with sweat pouring down our necks. I learned so much from my mom, mostly my frugality! Anything that was free was the best thing to can. We would get a bushel of pears not good enough for most people but perfect for us to can in jars with juice. For those unfamiliar with canning, it does not involve cans! It is a home processing method to preserve foods. Once sealed and heated in a pressure cooker for non-acid food or a water bath for high acid foods, they did not need refrigeration and were good for years. Every farm wife was proud when she had a pantry of canned foods. Our jars also filled the bomb shelter in case of nuclear attack. Green beans were processed in the pressure cooker, an old one without any safety locks. Later, as a young mom, I got a phone call from a woman screaming, "I'm burned, I'm burned!" I threw my children in my car and raced to my mom's house on the other side of town. She had opened the pressure cooker before the pressure had gone down, and boiling water had roiled down her front. Her shirt and fiberfill bra were melted into her breasts. I dunked a towel into cool water and wrapped it around the top of her, almost carried her to the car, and raced to Hunt Hospital. They tried to stop me, yelling "insurance information," but I was a lioness for my mom that day. I raced through the lobby with her until I saw an empty bed and put her on it, as I yelled "burn victim, going into shock." The doctors rushed in and were fantastic! Mom spent a few days in the hospital and was sent home with instructions for my dad to change the dressings. She developed water blisters that held a quart of water and scars that remained painful for years. Mom stopped canning soon after. Looking back, my sisters and I think that may have been the beginning of early Alzheimer's for her, as she had never made the mistake of opening her pressure canner too early. Although I teach canning at our local Topsfield Fair, I did not start using a pressure canner until they had safety devices. It is impossible to open them now until they cool. But I am an avid canner. It's an excellent way to be more sustainable and to know exactly what is going into the food your family eats. My children grew up watching me can and have many memories, such as helping grind hot peppers! My granddaughter was interested in learning and won a first place ribbon at the fair for her relish, and I was not one of the judges!

⚜ HAIR ⚜

My mom always told me that I had the most beautiful hair as a toddler. Then she told me it all went wrong. She wanted to brighten the blond, so she bought a product called Blond-Ex that could be used on children. She put great emphasis in reporting that it said "for children" and was created to keep your hair pretty and blond. She said, with obvious guilt, that my hair was never the same after she applied it to my locks. What I remember is her cursing and fighting my very thick, kinky, curly, and coarse "dirty blond" hair a few years later. I really don't think the Blond-Ex did it; I think my toddler hair was replaced by hair that was probably more similar to my father's hair. My father kept his hair very short when he was our dad, but I saw pictures of him as a younger man with really thick hair. My mom lived much of her life with guilt about almost everything and blamed herself for my hair.

My hair refused to be tamed. My mom bought her own thinning shears, similar to scissors but with spaced teeth to cut evenly spaced small chunks of hair. This thinning initially seems to make your hair lie flatter, but as it grows out it puffs it out even more. It gave me a sort of Bozo the Clown look. My hair was really thick and naturally curly and coarse. Most people made the comment to my mom, "Where did that hair come from?" My sisters bragged that they didn't have that kind of hair, boasting that they had normal hair. My younger sisters, now in their sixties, still brag about that!

On my few overnight visits to my godmother's house in the French section of Salem, my hair was transformed into a delight of nice curls.

Jeanette would use "spoolies," rubber little cones that she would twirl the hair around and then snap into place to hold the curls until my hair dried. She sometimes finger-curled my hair too. I felt like a princess, as I was never fussed over at home. Jeanette also bought me a really indulgent and most beautiful First Communion dress that I will never forget. My "city" curls didn't last long after I went home to the country. The humidity turned my head into what appeared to be a dark blond afro.

Unfortunately, as I entered my teens, curly hair was not one bit in style. My friend Susan had hair that was in style, perfectly straight and silky smooth. I worked so hard to make my hair conform to the style of the sixties. I got straight looking "hay" from ironing it on the ironing board. The cows and horses were always a threat! I got fairly nice results from setting it on orange juice cans and sleeping on it all night, as it was so porous it took hours and hours to dry. It is amazing that you can actually get used to sleeping with juice cans all over your head. A wonderful product called Curl Free came out, and worked for a few months at a time. By sixteen I had a real job and could afford to buy it. Nothing worked better than strong straightening chemicals to tame your hair. The smell while applying it was horrid and the chemicals could not have been a good thing against my scalp. So my hair was in control for a short time. However, by then I had full breasts, a curvy body, and unique weird hair. I couldn't have been more different from my sisters. That's when I fully decided that to be different was not a bad thing; I just wanted to be me, the unique middle sister. Soon after, I just let my hair go its own way as I have done since!

In my family, I was convinced by all that I was the fat one.
Pictures tell a different story!

⚛ THE FAT ONE ⚛

When you have three sisters who are string beans, you can easily be labeled the "fat one." I spent most of my life thinking I was fat. Looking back at old photos, it is obvious that I was never fat, just much bigger than my sisters. Being the heaviest was much more obvious when standing next to my oldest sister, as she was very tall as well as thin. Not only was my cousin Roger the same age as I, but we also had similar childhood physiques. He and I were robust and rounder than our siblings, and not very tall.

It's a wonder that I wasn't any heavier, as my mother loved to bake the most delicious cakes. My sisters were not big on sweets, so Mom would say with pride, "At least Sandy loves my cakes." Our diets in the winter were not particularly healthy, although all homemade. We didn't eat fast food; even though McDonald's had just sold its millionth hamburger in 1958, we didn't have one in our town until years later. Our food was "slow" food long before that was considered a desirable thing. Often it had been canned in the summer. My mother's canned tomatoes were always the base for her spaghetti sauce, but she never thickened it, so it was so watery it often slipped right off the plate onto the floor. Bowls worked better for the dish—one bite of tomatoes and one bite of bare spaghetti! Usually, it had ground beef in it also, so that was another separate bite! Every supper included a meat, a starch, and an overcooked vegetable. It was what my father expected every evening at 5:30, and for the years when they both had jobs, it was up to us to start it. Breakfast was always very early for my dad, with Mom making the most perfect

Cream of Wheat, without one lump, for him every single day. We always liked the leftovers because as it got old it lumped up and we liked the lumps! My father had some serious ulcers and evidently they worsened with spices, so everything mom cooked was bland. Salt wasn't a problem, so everything was well salted, but that was about it. He also didn't tolerate pork, so the only pork we had was the special French-style ground pork and mashed potatoes stuffing in the Thanksgiving turkey. For years, every other Thanksgiving we would go to Uncle Eddie's house for dinner, and my father lamented that he missed his special stuffing. After a few years, we stayed home for dinner on holidays.

In the spring we were lucky to dig dandelions and have fresh greens. In the summer we had lots of fresh garden vegetables, but unfortunately, they were usually overcooked. My father also had poor teeth and then no teeth, so that could have also explained the almost chew-free food we were served. Even when he got false teeth, he rarely used them to eat. They were just for formal occasions like my wedding.

My cousin Roger tried to share some of the healthy concoctions he made as a child in the farmhouse kitchen. His mom, Aunt Opal, was into health foods. In the blender, Roger would mix milk right from the cow, entire eggs right from the chickens, and a few other things, like fruit, and drink it up. He said you had to drink it slowly, so the eggshells stayed toward the bottom. My cousins were never sick! We were all so hard working, that is probably why we didn't gain too much weight. But my younger sisters still consider me the "fat one!"

⚞ EARLY SHOWS ⚟

The year was 1963. It was a big day for Howe-Manning School. Advertised as Dance Day in the *Middleton News*, a small locally published paper probably delivered through the schools, it was an important day for me. I was a Scottish Sword Dancer and got to wear a swishy skirt.

Tuesday, May 28, over one hundred pupils would perform at the school. I was eleven years old. Mrs. Giannino, the gym teacher, taught us the dance. This was a wonderful school sponsored event and was taught during our gym class but performed for our parents in the evening. My mom might have even been there to watch! Although I remember little of the event, I can still picture, in my mind, pointing my toes and tapping on each side of the crossed swords on the floor, then rotating to the music to another set of swords. It was a joyous moment. Also mentioned in the paper, there was another event that spring at Howe-Manning School. The article states, "A very successful show, 'Dixieland Minstrel' was presented by the Middleton P.T.A.," reminding me that times have changed for the better in many ways. It does enlighten one that in 1963, our little town had not progressed into a very racially accepting or sensitive community. It would be a few more years before the first African American family moved into town, and they would not have a very easy time adapting. My son had a black friend for a year or two and I was so happy that his parents kept his home full of cultural items, were proud of their heritage, and educated their sons well about history. I have always been a cultural sponge, seeking out differences to celebrate. As for Middleton, the selectmen named a dirt road "125th Street," referring to a New York city address in a Black inner city community. They thought it funny as the very first Black family in town lived in a house at the start of the road. When the family decided to move back to Roxbury, my husband's family took in their eldest son so he could continue to go to Masconomet High. Tommy was like a brother to my in-laws' sons for years, but Masco wasn't easy for most of us from Middleton, and it was really hard for a Black kid! It was reassuring that at least the school personnel would finally understand that blackface minstrel shows were racist and not at all appropriate. Progress has come slowly!

᚛ FORTS ARE THE BEST! ᚜

The one thing my sisters and I did really well was build forts. The stand of trees between the Wennerburg house and ours had a clump of four forty-footers and a treehouse fit inside perfectly. The trees were down in a low spot at the level of the swamp, so although the fort was far off the ground, it wasn't much higher than our house, and my mom could see us very well from the side door! We made sure not to put any windows on that side!

Not content to make a standard fort, my sisters and I, on the rare day we all played together, kept going up until the fort was three stories high. My father was not happy to see his cans of three penny nails disappear. He really got mad only if we used up all his spikes. Between each floor was a square opening and a rope ladder to climb from one floor to the next. The bottom floor was the kitchen with a large can for a stove. We made a small wood fire in the can, had some type of old metal rack over it, and set a pan on top. We knew enough to set the stove on a metal milk crate so the floor of the fort didn't catch on fire. Oh, the joy of boiling corn and eating it in our fort, without an adult helping us or even knowing what we were doing. The fact that the corn was cow corn, obtained on a secret mission to the fields between Haswell Park and River Street, and extremely tough didn't matter. It was a joyous day! Other days we heated canned soup, which was never as much fun as cow corn.

My father didn't help us with our forts. We salvaged old plywood and two-by-fours from his scrap piles. We learned by trial and error, and found out that swaying trees offer a challenge to novice builders. Our forts would creak and shift a bit, but they never fell down. After the forts, admittedly unsightly structures, my father offered to build us a nice "playhouse" in the back yard. We restored the trees to their former glory, removing every nail and board. My father actually unbent the nails to use them again; he was very frugal. He built us a perfect and nice looking playhouse!

⚔ TERROR ⚔

Nothing evokes memories as well as sheer terror. That tense sickening feeling, the rare feeling of total loss of control, the feeling of being prey—all this and more come back when I remember that night. Over fifty years ago, it seems like it was just last night. Without a speck of embellishment, this event really happened.

My friend Debbie was a bit more mature than I, although a year younger. She lived with a much older sister and was exposed to Elvis hysteria and boy/girl dating drama. We loved our Barbie dolls and set up the playhouse, the shed my dad built behind the house, adjacent to the swamp, for a day and night of fun. The playhouse had comfortable metal slat bunks, a table and even a square hole in the floor with a bucket under it for middle of the night toilet calls. We never raised the wooden door over the bucket because we were more worried about a muskrat coming up through the hole than we were of having to hold our pee. I was getting older, and obviously my bladder was finally doing its job. The twelve-by-twelve foot shed had windows, but they didn't open, being just to let light in. It was almost mosquito proof. The door latch was the only weak point, but we never worried about anybody coming into our backyard. It was just a spike nail on the inside two-by-four with a rope looped through a hole in the door. The rope loop draped over the nail to keep the door closed. It did leave a bit of a gap, but only if pulled on from the outside. My little sisters would sometimes pull on it so they could yell through the gap, usually a goofy taunt of some sort. They didn't play with Barbie dolls. This was the first time Debbie got to sleep over in the playhouse.

My mother made us take the dog with us that night, as it was the first time a kid from down the street ever stayed over. Never worried before, she felt a bit more protective when a neighbor's child was involved in the camp-out. I truly believe that black Lab saved our lives.

It was late when we finally stopped talking and laughing, as pre-teens are so inclined to do. Debbie in the top bunk and I in the bottom, we had started to doze off when we heard a slight noise at the door. I could see her face looking over the side of the bunk toward the door, and my eyes bulged toward it too, able to clearly make out the widening gap as the moonlight shone through the window. Time froze as the door was pulled out about five or six inches. As a large hand moved into the gap, following the rope inward, the dog began to bark furiously. The hand retreated. Neither Debbie nor I could scream, as we were in shock or just pure terror. The big outside light mounted on the back of the house came on as we heard some brush crackling on the dark side of the shed facing the swamp side. We knew "he" was just on the other side of the wall and yet we couldn't move or speak. My mother's voice out of the bathroom window questioned, "Everything okay out there?" We couldn't answer. In my mind, I begged her to come out and check on us. But neither of us made a peep. If the perpetrator escaped out the back through the edge of the swamp while my mom was talking, we will never know. If he stayed there until much later, he didn't make any noise leaving. We know we didn't sleep all night. Both of us lay still, breathing shallow, eyes wide open, ears listening to hear him leave. We never heard another sound and the dog didn't start barking again.

In the first light of morning, Debbie, the dog, and I made a run for the house. My mother was up making my father's Cream of Wheat, and we both burst out in frantic details about the night of terror. My dad looked at mom and they said, almost in unison, "Nobody is sleeping out in the playhouse again." No hugs, no comfort, no words of understanding, no calling the cops. We went back out to the playhouse once the sun was high in the sky and, sure enough, there were large footprints in the muddy ground coming in and out from the path that traversed the edge of the swamp out to the road.

Every time I watch a silly teen horror movie, I am amazed how stupid the kids are. How they don't run, how they often go toward the "creatures," how they don't call the police; all this makes more sense to me after my night of being so dumb. I felt a similar terror a few years later when I went to the movies with my boyfriend and saw *Wait Until Dark*. The audience could feel the tension more than the blind woman character, as we knew what was in her house. I actually jumped out of my seat in the theater a few times. Andy, thinking I was being such a baby, enjoyed being my protector. I thank God that Mom had the intuition to make us take the dog with us to the playhouse that night. Our black Lab earned an extra treat the next day. He was two young girls' protector.

Debbie and I waited for the scuttlebutt among the kids in Haswell Park to include some joking about scaring us. It never did. In fact, those that heard about it were also afraid. All of us pre-teens lost a bit of innocence over this incident. The big bad world had intruded right into the sanctity of my back yard. It had to have been an adult or much older teen, and they didn't have any good intentions, we knew that. We had slept out in that playhouse, my sisters and I, many times and never had a problem. This was the first time a child from down the street had slept out with either my sisters or I and it wasn't a secret. It would have been better if we had kept our plans to ourselves.

☀ NATURE SAVES ☀

I now know that the woods were my church. I tried to be a good Catholic for my mom; it seemed important to make her happy. Where I found solace and peace was under a tree or even a bush in the woods. I do thank God that he provided me with close access to my refuge spots. As a child, walking the trail to my grandpa's house was a joy, spending entire days in the polliwog ponds and picking blueberries for hours was also a joy. In the woods it was quiet. In the woods, no matter how closed in the brush and trees were, there was always space. There was never space in our house. There was rarely, if ever, quiet in our house. As I became an obsessed reader, it became easier to block out the noise in the house. A good story would keep my mind locked into the book like nobody else in my family understood. I didn't often take my books into the forest; I preferred to read the surroundings. Sitting on a clump of brush or moss, I could study the ants moving about so industriously. Without any training or encouragement, I started to notice that I could figure out just what the wildlife had done during the night from the signs they'd left. Sunny days were glorious days when I could do nothing but lie on the ground, away from the world, recharging with what we now understand as solar power. It wasn't often that I had these opportunities, but I was much happier when I did.

Sometimes I felt that taking refuge in the woods truly saved my life, or at least my emotional well-being. When both my parents were working at the factory, Patsy and I were instructed to have supper on the stove when they arrived home. Patsy was quite a bully to me, and

I cried easily and could be very sensitive. Early on, Patsy decided she wasn't going to take turns getting the potatoes peeled and on the stove to boil. When I reminded her it was her turn and she had to do it, the only answer I got was a fist into my nose. With blood spurting from my nose, I ran for the woods. I'll never know how it would have turned out if I'd fought back, though I think I would have been seriously injured. She towered over me in height and had no compunctions about hitting in the face. We were so lucky to have woods close enough that I could see my parent's car from across the cleared field. I didn't return home until hours later, after they did. I told my mom, but she had already lost any control of Patsy. Although she yelled at her, we all knew her yelling had no effect on anybody anymore. After that, I got dinner ready every night and Patsy started going off with her friends, often not even returning for supper. Jeanne and Janet needed only each other, and they seemed to feel relief at having the daily job of filling the bulkhead with firewood all to themselves each afternoon. As the twins got older, they got a small horse. My dad built a small barn and they seemed very happy. I still spent my small amount of free time in the woods, but I was becoming so engrossed in the books I was reading, I would even read in the woods. I never felt unsafe hidden away under a small pine, behind a rock, or among all the blueberry bushes. I didn't understand how anybody could live in cities, how a person could survive without open space and nature. As an adult, walking around Cambridge and Boston was never comfortable for me. My children came with me to Lesley College just once. They were very distressed that they didn't have books to carry; I bought them each three heavy old used textbooks from a bin for a few dollars each. They proudly carried them around as if they were current students, prodigies at the ages of eight and ten!

⚜ DENTIST VISITS ⚜

We all went to the dentist regularly but I was always uncomfortable in the dentist office. Most visits involved him leaning far too much on my chest as he worked. He would sing me love songs. Creepy! My mother showed little concern when I gave her specifics, always telling me his prices were "cheap" and he did fix our teeth. I guess we couldn't afford a dentist who was socially appropriate. You get what you pay for!

When my father had to have all his teeth pulled, we all waited anxiously for months for new dentures to be made. My mother was so excited to have her handsome husband back again. Finally he came home, where we were all waiting for his smile. He didn't even have to smile before we could see the teeth! They were the biggest set of teeth any of us had ever seen on a small-headed person like my dad. The first words to come into our thoughts, as we whispered to each other, were "horse teeth." If we didn't look at each other or our mother's face we would have been able to suppress it, but we did and we couldn't. The laughter started and none of us could stop, not even my mother. Tears ran down our faces, and every time my mom tried to make a supportive comment, even she started laughing again. My poor father finally ran into the bathroom and took them out.

My mom made him go back, and the dentist somehow adjusted the set so they were a bit smaller. The fact that he should have made another set was never discussed. However, it was a rare occasion when my father would wear them. He couldn't comfortably eat with them. My mom insisted that he wear them for just a few occasions, such as my wedding. He would leave them in long enough for pictures. Without any teeth,

his face was a bit sunken. I really appreciated that he made the sacrifice for my mom and I, and he does look very handsome in my wedding
pictures, although he never really let a big smile come out!

As soon as I could, I found my own dentist, even though I had to use
my own money to pay him. I suppose having a dentist as repulsive and
inappropriate as we did really encouraged tooth brushing and good oral
care. Maybe that was my mother's reasoning!

⚡ MÉMÈRE COMES TO LIVE WITH US ⚡

We hadn't enjoyed our new small ranch house for very long when tragedy struck in the form of my father's mother having a severe stroke. My mom, having taken care of her own mother for many challenging years, still felt guilt at finally having her placed in the medical unit of Danvers State Hospital, where she died within a few months. Although Mémère would need full-time nursing care, my mother could not say no to my father. He wanted his mother to live with us, and there was no medical insurance for a good nursing home, although some relatives said Père, as we called my grandfather, could have afforded it. My mom agreed to take her into our home from the hospital, where they had given her no hope for recovery or rehabilitation. Of course, Père was elated, as was my father. Mémère would have personal round-the-clock care in our home by our already busy mother. She didn't have any formal nursing training, but she knew how to bathe invalid people and change soiled beds. Mémère was half the size of my Nana (Mom's mother), so Mom felt confident she could lift her. The town visiting nurse would come once a week to tell my mother what a good job she was doing, and what a saint she was!

So, all four of us girls were moved into a 10 by 12 foot room, the largest bedroom in the house, we were reminded. With two bunk beds side by side and two bureaus, there was not much room left and no privacy whatsoever! I was elected to have the top bunk. I presume because I didn't wet my bed anymore, Patsy felt comfortable below me. Jeanne and Janet had the other set of bunks. It was also the end of having friends come into our house to play!

Mémère was paralyzed on one entire side. She had lost all speech except the "Hail Mary" in French, which she would scream anytime she wasn't sleeping. It was as if she were stuck in some long penance after going to the confessional at church. She was totally incontinent. One arm had incredible strength, and she used it to reach under her and grab feces, which she would smear on any surface within arm's length, usually the wall beside the bed. If my mother was close and unaware, the feces would be flung at her. The amount of dirty laundry was enormous, and we still had the old wringer washer in the basement. She had to be hand fed every meal, and during the feeding her good arm would have to be tied down or she would knock every spoonful of the pureed mush across the room. My mother was very attentive to her, taking pride that in those long months of being bedridden, Mère never developed bedsores. The house almost always smelled of either feces or a cover-up deodorizer. In our small house, the sounds and smells of serious sickness permeated every nook and cranny. Her care stretched into a year, as Mère's heart was very strong. Her voice also remained strong, and the Hail Mary scream was part of our lives for a long time.

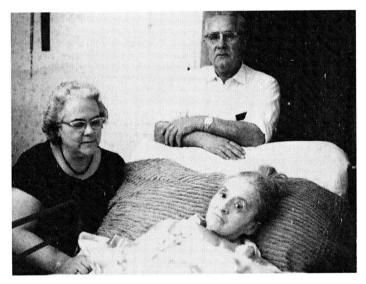

After my father's mother had a stroke, my mother cared for her. It was a difficult time for all of us. My godmother, Jeanette, on the left, my grandfather on the right, his wife, Mere, in bed.

Roger, like a brother to me growing up, could drive anything.
It was a treat for him to "play."

❧ HELPING ROGER ❧

When we were little, it was always, "If you are looking for Roger, look for Sandy." We were the same age and as close as siblings; actually, some years we were a lot closer than I was to my sisters. As the first-born son in his family, Roger had to work almost every waking moment. He attended school only when his father didn't have a job that needed to be done on the farm. He was registered at St. Joseph's School in Salem, just as his sisters were, so the town school authorities didn't know he wasn't attending regularly. When he did attend, the nuns really liked him. As he wasn't able to learn to read through any known conventional teaching, they had him sweeping the floors and doing custodial duties. I am sure he had some severe reading disabilities that were never addressed in school. Roger could do almost anything but read and write. He was very smart. He also may have had undiagnosed ADHD as, unless motivated, he could not attend to academic tasks or sit still very long. His daily life at home was becoming harder; he worked like a grown man every day. He was just a pre-teen when his father ran over his leg with a huge dump truck. He was in a cast for what seemed like a long time, but the leg never really healed properly, and Roger had huge scars running the length of it. He said he actually feared for his life, as battles with his father were becoming worse. He also feared the school authorities would find out he wasn't attending school and he would be sent to reform school, or the farm, as it was known. He asked me to help him run away at the age of fourteen or fifteen. I had saved a lot of my babysitting money and gave it all to him.

I'm sure it wasn't that much, but it was enough. We planned for his escape and he was off.

I got one postcard from him, written just legibly enough to get through the mail and be delivered to me. I was so happy he was safe, getting rides from long haul truckers, and arriving in Corpus Christi, Texas, where he planned to stay awhile. Roger worked farms and became much physically bigger and stronger, until he felt he could stand up to his father. He also turned sixteen, the legal age that you could quit school in Massachusetts. When he returned, his goal was to get his license and a set of wheels. He knew how to operate cars, trucks, bulldozers, and farm equipment, so driving wasn't an issue. The wheels would also be the easy part; he could change out a motor and get almost any vehicle running. The license was much harder. We worked for months on the driver's education questions, and the only reason he could concentrate was because he knew he had to have a license. Finally, I thought he was ready, and he took an oral test and passed.

Roger and I had a few more adventures before we went in different directions—those stories can be found elsewhere in this book. He had such a good heart, remembering me when my grandfather's house was ready to be torn down, calling me to come and get mementos, such as footprints Patsy and I had made in the cement walkway. Roger married and had beautiful children. I enjoyed taking his two youngest from his second wife camping, and we still stay in touch. Roger never could shake off the ghosts of his childhood, though. He had challenges no child should ever have to face. He worked hard all his life and he passed away too early. I miss him, as frustrating as he could be, and he was like the brother I never had.

❧ PÈRE AND I ❧

During Mémère's illness, my father decided that one of us kids had to go over to Père's house to bring in his wood every afternoon. I volunteered immediately! Having such a strong olfactory sense, I knew it would be better than being in my house with the smells of human excrement everywhere. Being so young, I would have to walk to my grandfather's, and I knew the way through the woods very well. If it got dark by the time I left, I would take the road home, down Route 114 to Haswell Park. If Mom needed bologna from Leo's package store for Dad's lunch, I would have to take the road home too. Père lived in a small white house across from Richardson's ice cream, near the former location of Kuells Market. Although his mailbox was on Route 114, he had a nice long driveway that circled his house and was lined with the most spectacular hydrangeas I have seen anywhere. I called them "snowball bushes"! As I left my house, I went through the field adjacent to the Blais farm and around the old Richardson family cemetery. I never walked through the cemetery when alone! After cutting through many great blueberry picking spots, I then headed uphill and skirted the back of the Whites' Christmas tree farm. Dropping into a deep gully, where there were some wet cranberry bush areas, I followed a worn trail that led to a huge pine, dubbed the "smoking tree" a few years later. Not that the tree smoked! It was the rite of passage for every neighborhood teen to try smoking under that tree. After that, the trail climbed uphill and joined a more worn path that led past three sheds belonging to my grandfather. All these sheds were exciting, having the best stuff stored in them. Picture boxes of finger cots, little rubber finger covers, which later we would joke looked like condoms for elves. They were finger protection for working on light bulbs and other tasks at Sylvania. Père had worked there during mid-life and had accumulated some really neat things. Interestingly, my mom had worked at the Sylvania plant in Ipswich at the end of World War II. She knew what these finger thingies really were!

Père would often meet me outside. Although Mère had never seemed good company in my childish eyes, I'm sure he was lonely without her. My cousin Carol is a few years older than me and has some memories of playing checkers with Mémère long before her stroke. She also remembered her kneeling on a hard wooden chair to say the rosary for hours and refusing a cushion from Père when he would try to make it easier for her. As I worked bringing in his wood, he'd help a bit, although he was getting along in years. Sometimes he would need something in the basement, and he would let me go down there with him. I will always love the damp, musty smell of old rock-walled basements. I especially wanted his Hawaiian coconut head decoration and can clearly visualize it hanging from the ceiling just beyond the steep stairs. I never asked for anything, though. His stories were gift enough.

Père wouldn't start telling me stories until the dog was given his food, a huge pan of hot bread in a broth sitting on the hot wood stove. The predominate smell was of smoldering apples, as he always had a cut apple half lying on the hot stove plates. The kitchen was actually the "everything" room, and I never ventured beyond that. It had a huge table just as you entered on the right and a big wood cookstove centered on the left wall. Opposite was the sink and counters. It was always eighty degrees cozy in that room and he loved to talk. It was really special because when he was with my dad, he spoke only in French. With me, he talked in English and told me stories I had never heard from my father.

We fast danced to sixties music and he jokingly held his heart. I loved him so much and could not ever imagine he would be killed just one year after this party.

⚘ MÉMÈRE PASSES ON ⚘

At home one day, I noticed that the Hail Marys had stopped. My sisters were outside, my mother was doing laundry in the cellar, and I was alone upstairs. I went to the doorway of the room where Mère lay. She was quiet. I was not even in my teens yet, and I just stood there watching the chest of my French grandmother. It wasn't moving. She seemed at peace for the first time since her stroke. I called to Mom, and she sent me running to the little rented house on the farm next door, where our nurse friend lived. Janet came down and pronounced her deceased. My mother called Père and my father. My mother shared in their grief, but what I noticed was the incredible sense of relief, of calmness, that came over my mother. She had nothing to feel guilty for; she had done more than enough. As the visiting nurses always told her, she was a saint.

Long after Mère was gone, I continued to help out Père and enjoyed every minute of it. If I mentioned one of my grandfather's stories to my father, he would dismiss it as the ramblings of an old man, but I knew Père was sharing important parts of his life. He rarely, if ever, told anyone the story of his first child. But I liked and listened to his stories without comment. In front of the stove in the kitchen one day, he began to talk very quietly of her. He said she was just a toddler. His wife, Marie, had put the metal diaper pot on the stove and got it to boiling before she moved it to the edge to start filling it with soiled diapers. The pot wasn't big enough and a few diapers hung down the side. As she went back to the bedroom to make sure she had gotten all the dirty diapers, evidently the toddler reached up just enough to pull on a hanging diaper edge. The bucket, on the very edge and slightly unbalanced, fully tipped toward the child, pouring boiling water over her. She died of her injuries, and Marie never allowed anybody to speak of her again. Years later, she birthed two sons, Leopold and Antonio, my father and uncle.

My cousin told me she had once seen a picture at Mère's house of a little girl, but then it disappeared. She also wondered if this accident could be why Mere punished herself by kneeling on a wooden chair to say the rosary. Père told me that his wife, Marie, had never shown loving warmth to the boys. He said she never showed affection to him either; she seemed to have no love left in her soul after the deadly accident. He was not allowed to speak of it. Only he knew that all her motherly affections were buried deep with their little girl, and that she held tremendous guilt inside—guilt that a million Hail Marys would not lessen.

Years later, when we celebrated his seventy-eighth birthday, Père tried some modern dances with me; he was such a good sport and lots of fun. He would also come down to the ice pond on the farm and watch us skate. Père drove his car to Salem, with my dad telling us he sometimes made the whole trip without shifting gears. There were many fun celebrations at his house after Mère was gone. Although I heard hushed talk between my mom and dad about Père seeing a doctor and being told some bad news about his health, little did I ever think that he would be gone in 1969. He was hit by a red dump truck while getting his mail on Route 114. Saturday, the eighth of November, was a sad day for all of us. They never caught the hit-and-run driver, but a truck in a small town on what was at the time not a very busy road, shouldn't have been hard to find. I always wondered if Père, having watched his wife suffer for so long, made sure he never went through any illness like that. Maybe he deliberately stepped in front of a truck. We will never know, as there was never much of an investigation. My father felt the town knew but did not want to officially "find" the driver. It wouldn't bring his father back. And my father really disliked conflict.

My French Catholic Godmother, Jeanette, gifted me the most exquisite dress. I felt so special. It was the beginning of my Catholic childhood.

☙ BEING CATHOLIC ❧

The best thing about being Catholic is that we didn't have to work on Sundays. I think that was the only reason my father practiced Catholicism, although all the French immigrants were Catholic. If we were lucky, he would take us with him to St. Joseph's Catholic Church in Salem on Sunday mornings. The mass was all in French so we didn't understand a word of it. We were used to that, because earlier it had been recited in Latin, and we didn't understand a word of that either. The early mass in Salem was the shortest anywhere. It started at 6 a.m., or close to that because it was dark when we drove there. My father never did the "extras" that make you a good Catholic. He didn't go to confession or communion. Sometimes we thought he was sleeping, but he was always awake when it was over. We got out as the sun was coming up, about a half hour later. It was a beautiful church with a lot of statues. I do remember that the ride to church and home again was always a pleasant time with Dad; he seemed relaxed and was actually playful, with us grabbing each other's knees, yelling "monkey bites." This was as close to affection as my dad ever showed.

When we were old enough to make our first communion, we had to go to Sunday school. It was fun because a bunch of us got to walk from Howe-Manning to St. Agnes by ourselves. Father Donohue shifted from saying mass in Latin to saying it in English, but by then there was something wrong with his throat or voice so we still couldn't understand that much of the service. I do know that when it was time to make your first confession, you had to have some sins. I always said, "I disobeyed my father and mother," although I never really did. I think that was the stock phrase when you couldn't think of anything else. Once, I actually said, "I read a dirty magazine," but if I did, I'm sure it must have been my big sister's. My mother should have confessed that she said bad words, because she was always saying "shit." It was really scary being in that confessional box and trying to remember the lines and what the priest told you to say to get rid of all those sins. Three Hail Marys and one Our Father was almost always my penance, and of course we were convinced the priest would know if we didn't say them.

My father was smart to skip the extras. He got into an argument with another worker at Parker Brothers one time and didn't speak to the guy for over twenty years. I do believe he retired without ever having spoken to him again. So, he missed the forgiveness lesson; that is for sure! He was a good provider, didn't beat us, was a good husband, and he went to church every Sunday. He did call the Sears & Roebuck catalog his bible, so he could honestly say he read his bible every day.

We never missed church. We didn't eat meat on Fridays during Lent. I always gave up something I would really miss for the entire forty days of Lent. One year, I had succeeded in not eating any candy or sweets until almost Easter, when Patsy tricked me into eating an M&M before I thought about it. She knew I was determined to please God, and she ruined it! I always wondered what Patsy said in the confessional booth.

As teens, we had to attend the Catholic education program called CCD. It was taught by really handsome young "brothers" from the seminary. I really enjoyed listening to their teachings one night a week. I was such a goody two shoes! Most of the girls hung out in the parking lot, making out with their boyfriends. Most of the boys outside were much older and not Catholic, but they knew when to come around. Cars were rocking and windows were steamed. The parking lot on Boston Street next to St. Agnes Church was a hotbed of young adolescents with raging hormones. It gave new meaning to the teaching of "love one another."

MY MOM REMEMBERS CHURCH
⚞ DURING HER CHILDHOOD ⚟

It was a long walk home from church at St. Rose in Topsfield. My father, Henry, would drive my mother, brother, and I to the church and drop us off every Sunday morning. The Old Linebrook Road house we lived in was less than five miles away from the church, closer than going to Ipswich center. "Kate, I will pick you up in an hour," was what my father said every week to my mom. But he never remembered to pick us up. It was a long walk home.

☆ MASCONOMET ☆

Masconomet Regional School was built in Boxford in 1958 and was for students from Boxford, Topsfield, and Middleton. It was named for the *sagamore* (paramount chief) of the Agawams that had lived in Essex County. Initially, the Boxford/Topsfield building committee sought out other towns to join the school. A top pick was Lynnfield, but it was not interested. Georgetown didn't have enough money. After a few other towns also showed no interest in joining with Topsfield and Boxford, Middleton was finally invited to join, forming the Tri-Town school community. Middleton had been sending its high school students to Holten High in Danvers for freshman year and then to Salem High for the sophomore and junior years. These students became the first graduating class of Masconomet in 1960. They were proud to have their own high school. The superintendent-principal was Mr. Julius H. Mueller, and the dedication of the school was attended by Reverend Donohue of St. Agnes Church in Middleton and Reverend Silvius of the Episcopal Mission of Topsfield and Boxford. The first official day was September 14, 1959, and it was recorded that 765 students attended the six-year regional school that year.

I entered Masco in 1963 with excitement. I was an avid reader and loved to learn. Already wanting to be a teacher, I had high hopes for the future. At eleven, I was on the younger side, as my birthday was in October, but I was maturing fast. There were other girls who already had breasts, but that wasn't yet the norm. Many of the boys from Middleton seemed older and tougher than others of the same age in junior high.

As retention was still used extensively in Middleton, the ones sprouting beards were chronologically older! My mom had to buy some of our school clothes, so we didn't have expensive or numerous outfits, but they were clean and nice enough. Being in school was very different from hanging out in my neighborhood. In Haswell Park, the kids were close, for better or for worse. At Masco, the world was so much bigger, so different, and there seemed to be no time for relationships or even deep conversation. It was all I could do to find my way to each class; the day was filled with bells and movement, even at lunch. For me, lunch wasn't a time to socialize. I was usually starving and have always been a slow eater, yet I love food. I wanted to finish every morsel of that formed ball of sticky rice with chicken à la king all over it! Seriously, I loved school food. But I didn't like watching the clock and trying to hurry as I ate. My most prevalent memory of junior high was being rushed all the time.

Right from the start, math was my weakest subject. Reading and writing was a strength, although not much more than an average strength at Masconomet. I would have flunked the sewing semester of home economics if my mother had not sewn my apron for me. The teacher said I could finish it at home after I broke the third sewing machine! I excelled during the cooking semester, of course, mostly because I liked to eat so much. Physical education was a total embarrassment, but that was probably true for most girls experiencing their first shower room dramatics. I was extremely modest—not a good trait when the towels are half the size of your body. I wasn't heavy but was developing fast and started my period at thirteen in school. It was a good thing we had health or puberty education, because my mother never had that "talk" with me. It was also a good thing the school had free pads if you needed them. Tampons had been invented in 1929 by Dr. Earle Haas, although there is mention of tampon-type items in ancient history. Seven years later, Gertrude Tenderich bought the patent and this savvy business-woman founded Tampax. As I lived in Massachusetts, it is amazing that, even after Tampax moved its operations to a textile mill in my very own state back in 1941, I didn't know what tampons were. During World War II, sales exploded as women entered the workforce or military service. I was never offered the option of tampons, and for the next six years, I would endure that huge bulge of a pad between my thighs for a week every month. Maybe I thought tampons would take my virginity away, maybe I was afraid, or maybe I just couldn't afford them. I just know I didn't have them to use. The pad holder with clips in front and back was a nightmare too. It was a strap around your waist, with one dangling strap, front and back, with metal clips. The ends of the pad looped into the clips. I complained only once to my mom, and she answered with, "I had to use cloth diapers and wash them out every night to reuse over and over. Think about a diaper balled up between your legs; those pads you have to use are nothing!" My mom spoke of her sacrifices and hardships like a badge of courage. She had no sympathy for her four daughters! When I started playing field hockey in the eleventh grade, it was a blessing that Stayfree Maxi Pads with adhesive strips had been invented. They came on the market in 1969, and I was working and making enough money to buy my own!

In junior high, it seemed almost all students took the same subjects. There wasn't a big distinction among levels of study, at least not that I was aware of. At the end of eighth grade, when we were required to pick subjects for high school, things started to change. My parents, especially my mother, had strong opinions. "Take the easiest courses—that's what I did—and you get the same diploma. It doesn't matter what your grades are as long as you pass. I got my diploma with all Cs." Hoping for a different story from the school advisors, I was met with almost the same message. I was told, "Business courses would be best for you." I didn't want to be a secretary; in fact, I almost flunked typewriting in junior high, and I still use only two fingers.

I made my father happy by taking French, until he found out this Parisian French was nothing like the French Canadian dialect he spoke. I was so hoping to understand the conversations my father and Père would have that we weren't supposed to be listening to. I asked the teacher why the French I was trying to learn at Masconomet was not more similar to my father's. I was told, "I teach Parisian French, not poor farmers' dialect." I lost enthusiasm for French in the language lab, which stressed me out so much I couldn't think, but at least I ended up with a C, so my mom was happy. I didn't listen to the advisors who tried to help me pick my high school courses; I took college prep classes and have never regretted it. Many other Middleton kids listened and they regretted it very much.

When I was in junior high, a huge uproar took place. In 1963, a Masconomet staff member, either a department chairperson or principal, made some derogatory remarks at a public school committee meeting. These remarks were published in the local newspaper and many local townspeople vividly remember the hurt and anger these remarks caused. The students of Middleton were referred to as "ragamuffins," and the comment implied that Masconomet could be a great school without them. However the remark was stated, the word "ragamuffin" stayed in the heads of all the Middleton kids and their parents. *The Middleton News* ran a full-page editorial page printing the many comments parents sent in and demanded an apology from the administrator and teacher. Over fifty years later, when I asked about their experience at Masconomet, almost all the Middleton adults I queried spoke first of being called a "ragamuffin."

A half-hearted public apology did little to quell the anger and disappointment Middleton parents now had for the Masconomet staff. It seemed to create less motivation and more rebelliousness in students already lacking a sense of worth and direction. Many of the kids from Middleton accepted a schedule that included three or four study halls a day, with only the state-mandated classes. Even then, several programs were instituted to ensure Middleton kids were not taking up space in the classrooms. Some students from Boxford and Topsfield also fit into the school's "under-motivated" category, and it was interesting to watch how they gravitated together with some Middleton kids. Instead of trying to excite these kids with more creative learning within the college prep courses, special classes were created for them. My future husband left for a vocational school when he had more study halls than classes. My older sister dropped out as soon as she turned sixteen. My younger sisters were pushed into the work-study program.

It was easy to convince parents with only a high-school education and a life of factory work that it would be best for their children to enter a work-study program. The state mandates would be met with

EDITORIAL

It is my opinion that to properly educate our children we must have teachers in the school system whose character is above reproach, for in their hands lie the task of molding the minds of children.

There is no place in the system for radicals, or persons who have any deep prejudices. The world today is troubled enough with the small minds of small men.

We cannot compromise our children's education. We should accept nothing less than the resignation of one---.
Richard P. Merrill.

COMMENTS (cont.)

" he should not have said that, even if he felt that way, this is no way for a teacher to talk. I would like to see him suspended, but do not wish his family to suffer for his mistake. "

Name withheld on request.

" he should be suspended, the children are very upset, many are afraid they may get him next year. I am very surprised a comment like that came from a man of education. "

Mrs. Evelyn Kingsvater
School Street,
Middleton

"It is too bad that a person of such high standing should belittle himself by such an ambiguous statement. "

Mrs. Ann Woodbury
Liberty Street,
Middleton

" The Lawrence Eagle quotes Webster's definition of Mr. Merrill's choice word " ragamuffin, " for us. "

" I also would like to quote Mr. Webster on a decription of Mr. Merrill. " SNOB; 1) One who blatantly imitates, fawningly admires, or vulgarly seeks association with those who he regards as his superiors.

2) One who by his conduct makes evident that he sets excessive store by rank, wealth, or social eminence, to the detriment of merit.

Choice number 2 is a shoe that should fit our eminent teacher very comfortably.

Mrs. June Schlichting
Essex Street,
Middleton

"As a kindergarten teacher, I know that this can exists in any group but to condemn a whole town, is in very poor taste. The town should have a public apology

even though the harm has been done. "

Mrs. Virginia Donovan
Johns Avenue,
Middleton

"this man is not qualified to teach in such a lovely school as Mascon not especially the children of Middleton, a town that boasts of some of the nicest people and homes in the area."

Mr. Joseph Picariello
Boston Street,
Middleton

" I feel sorry for him in a way. His type of thinking exposes him for what he is and as such leaves much to be desired. "

Mr. Raymond Dansereau
Lake Street,
Middleton

mini-courses—translation, easy for any kid to pass! My sisters and many other students, almost all from Middleton, would leave school every day at noon. The school found them jobs at local factories; for my sisters and dozens of others it was HotWatt in Danvers. They were taught assembly-line wiring tasks. My sisters were never students with special needs; however, these types of jobs now usually go to people with specific disabilities. Those students with cognitive impairments who excel in repetitive visual and manual motor skills often do well with this type of work. These Middleton students had neither special needs nor disabilities. Yet their "advisors" highly recommended this "work-study" program, which actually trained them to become a factory worker and nothing else! My sisters completed high school with all half days, and, as my mother noted, their diplomas look the same as every other student's!

I specifically remember being upset that the required "history" course, for example, was condensed into a mini-course on witchcraft. I tried to tell my sisters that they may not qualify to get into a college after graduation, but my concerns fell on deaf ears. My parents thought that was just fine, as both my twin sisters had been able to buy a nice car soon after they were sixteen. Other Middleton kids had experiences that were more disturbing. Middleton students were often verbally bullied, although it was not recognized as such, and most Middleton parents just told their kids to "deal with it." I have been told so many stories that they could fill a book, and the tellers would like me to include them all, but many of the verbal comments are too intense to repeat. Some of those who shared their stories were from Boxford, as many of the children from farm families experienced the same treatment. These kids were not often physically bullied because, along with being "poor, dirty ragamuffins" or "hicks," they were tough! And they were often the young men who volunteered with courage to go off and fight for this country.

The sense of self-esteem for many of the Middleton young men came almost exclusively from shop. Whether it was wood shop, metal shop, or automotive shop, those boys were happy there. The shop teachers could appreciate the unique intelligence and life experience they had and could ignore most acts of bravado. They hung out in the lower hallway that led to the junior high, the only place that, it you weren't a jock, you felt accepted. If you happened to be a jock, especially a good football player, none of this applied. You were respected for your athletic prowess and academic help was offered to make sure your eligibility to play was not at risk. For the most part, few Middleton kids played sports. Many had after-school jobs and little money for training and equipment. This was one of the areas where I became an exception. Never a star, but a player!

Both my parents worked at Parker Brothers when I was in high school. They had no idea what I did with my time after school and were fine with that as long as supper was started when they got home at five-thirty. I knew an older girl who lived on a side street off my road; Ruthie was an excellent gymnast. One of the girls hanging with the tough Middleton crowd, Norma, also played basketball. There were only a few Middleton girls playing sports, but I was never one to be the same as most. I decided I wanted to play field hockey and tried out. I made JV the first year but played varsity in my senior year. I think seniors had to be put on the varsity team! I took the late bus home every night as a junior, before I got a car, getting home by 5 p.m. in time to start supper. The girls on the varsity team were nice people and fantastic field hockey players, but we lived in different worlds. They were all friends outside of school too. I usually sat alone on the team bus to away games and was fine with that. Although I noticed, it never bothered me that nobody was ever at my games, either home or away, to watch me play. I didn't expect it, as my parents had to work. I was proud to wear my red skirt, hockey socks, and shin protectors and I always tried to give my best. I'm sure the other local kids I hung with sometimes thought I was lame and nerdy! It was not considered cool to play sports in a red skirt with bloomers, the Masco uniform. I wasn't really good, I wasn't bad, and I was never a star. I was a loner within the team, but the other girls were always nice to me. I still have my red sports letters, thick wool red Ms!

☆ FIRST REAL BOYFRIEND ☆

I honestly can't remember where we first met. This is particularly disappointing for me as we ended up spending almost three years together! Before I met Andy, I had friends in school and in the neighborhood. But now I was fourteen and was so very different from everybody else. I often had my head in a book, losing myself in mystery novels during every bit of free time I was allowed up to this point. During elementary school, I had hung around with kids from down the street, and in school I had a good friend in Cheryl Bowes, whose mother was the school nurse. I got to spend some time at Cheryl's house, a pleasant, newer ranch on Wennerburg Road. I vividly remember riding in Mrs. Bowes's car. Every time she had to apply the brake, she reached over with her arm stretched across both of us in the front seat to make sure we didn't go forward and hit the dashboard. Cars didn't have seat belts in the early fifties, but Mrs. Bowes would protect us! This was the sweetest, most kind gesture I had encountered during my childhood, along with the life-changing summer with Mrs. Lewis. Cheryl and her sweet mom were too good to believe, and I was a child in another world during the years we were friends. But elementary school years were soon behind me, and I stopped hanging with Cheryl in junior high. The boys in junior high, with the exception of a most beautiful blond boy whom I was quite enamored with, didn't interest me. The blond never even looked at me, although I do believe he was the subject of my entire first diary! I really wish I had kept that diary. Then, somehow, I met Andy, a young man who some, including my parents, considered to be from the wrong side of the tracks! It's so funny to say that, as my parents didn't realize most of the Middleton kids were considered to be from the wrong side of the tracks, or maybe the wrong side of Route 95, as the high school was on the other side.

Andy was beautiful! He had smooth bronze skin and sculpted cheekbones. He had muscles in all the right places. He had straight, silky, dark black hair that he wore long and brushed to one side over his dark eyes. He had the most magnificent smile and nice teeth. Andy had just finished a year in reform school where he was routinely beaten and kicked in the head so many times that I could feel the scars under his thick hair. Evidently, Andy had a problem with authority. It was never clear why he was sent to the "the Farm" except that he was often truant from school. After he was released from the Lawrence Reformatory, he never returned to school. As soon as you turned sixteen, you did not have to go to school. He carried himself with a tough persona that intimidated many. I am sure he learned how to be a survivor: hide your feelings and be tougher than everybody else. His mom was rarely seen around town and his dad never seemed to emerge from a back room in the house.

I may have met Andy while hanging with my older sister's friends. We had a lot of places to hang out that most adults were never aware of, and I tagged along with Patsy's friends often, although I was a few years younger than most of them. I was quiet, more of an observer, and strong in my conviction that I would avoid sexual relationships. I really didn't think I would be a better person; I just didn't want to be what other people expected me to be. The phrase "Blais girls" became both a complimentary term that reflected the beauty of the sisters but also hinted at promiscuity. I also didn't smoke, although I tried it a few times under the smoking tree and at the Middleton Drive-in. It made me dizzy and I was obsessed with always being in control of my thoughts and actions. I tried drinking beer and I couldn't stomach the taste of it. I would share a bit of Boone's Farm at the drive-in, but never enough to get tipsy! I wasn't cool or even very pretty, although I did have big breasts, and that counted for a lot in the sixties. Other girls had much bigger breasts and some really suffered in sixth grade when some of the older boys looked at nothing else but a girl's chest. In junior high school, the seventh and eighth grade at Masconomet, many girls were more attractive and had much better bodies than I did. I was always different, never succumbing to peer pressure to smoke, drink, or engage in sex. I also liked people who were different. A new student started riding our school bus; although moving from a city close to Middleton, his family was originally from Italy. A skinny boy with skin so white it seemed almost translucent, he was very handsome in a unique sort of way. Nobody else would talk to Vito in the first few weeks, so I sat with him on the bus and made conversation. To this day he tells me I was the only person who was nice to him when he first moved to Middleton. Vito did finally make townie friends, joining the "tougher" Middleton kids and losing his uniqueness during the journey from loner to groupie.

Andy, as far as I can remember, was never "reformed" by societal standards, yet I saw a young man who craved love and affection under a tough exterior. I saw something very different in him and wanted to get to know him better.

Nobody ever understood our relationship. My parents, as they told me years later, thought that by not forbidding me from seeing him I would eventually move on. They never thought it would be years later! Andy's friends were confused. Here was the toughest guy in town dating a wuss! I was a wimp who had her head in a book most of the time. The other girls in his crowd were very streetwise, smoking and swearing while doing the least amount of schoolwork possible. Some had even dropped out of school. The girls didn't trust me, hiding their cigarettes whenever I walked into the school bathroom, thinking I could be a snitch! Andy and I reinvented our world, just the two of us, without a care in the world what anybody else thought. We held hands as we walked around town. We would buy a pizza at the sub shop in Middleton Square, walk down Lake Street and have a picnic on the ledge below a house-sized boulder overlooking Middleton Pond. We rode with a bunch of older kids to the beach a few times, and while they all stood around looking cool and smoking, we buried each other in the sand, laughing and frolicking like two little kids. Our favorite thing to do was to walk behind my house, across the cow pasture to the bigger sloping grass fields that went all the way to River Street. This pasture wasn't grazed some years and had tall, soft grass; we would lie down and roll over and over to the bottom of the hills. We always sat outside in nature, talking for hours and hours, yet he never talked of his father. Andy told me enough to know that it was not a good relationship. I didn't pry. He idolized his oldest brother, the one doing a bit of time in jail, but he never told me what he did to end up there. He also loved and respected his other brother and his sisters. We only went to his house once, and I stood just inside the door. It was so dark I couldn't even see where to sit if I had been offered a chair. Andy put on a tough façade to survive, but he was sweet and childlike with me. We found an old car way down back in the cow pasture on the Blais farm and would "make-out," but he never pressured me to go "all the way." We would sometimes double-date with an older friend and his date. We would almost always go parking on one of the backwoods dirt roads. Andy and I would sit for only a few minutes before jumping out of the car and heading for a pretty spot in the woods, not wanting to witness another couple having sex. We did get to a few movies and shared nice Christmas gifts that year. I know Andy bought my gift at the Middleton Drugstore, as he had to walk everywhere. It was a basket set of Jean Naté. I got to JJ Newbury's in Peabody and got him an Irish knit sweater, not made in Ireland but affordable for me. If anybody could make an Irish knit sweater look absolutely stunning, it was Andy!

We did sometimes hang out with a group that included a really nice couple, Paulie and Neil. Neil was also unconventional as he was older, and I believe already out of school. I do know we went to see the movie *Wait Until Dark* with them and had a great time. In the 1968 yearbook, which I bought as a freshman, Paulie wrote a long passage that filled most of the inside front cover. She wrote, "You and Andy have made the cutest couple. Hang on to him, he's okay. I could never picture Andy on a picnic, down the park on the swings or even flying a kite. You two really make a good pair, one as crazy as the other. Andy wouldn't go on picnics and fly kites if he didn't care a lot. Don't forget all the fun we had up the square. Good luck in the future, I think we all need it." She signed it, "Love always, Paulie" and wrote "Andy+ Sandy, Paulie+ Neil" next to it. I think the reason she says we needed luck was that the Vietnam War with the draft was going on and Neil may have been eighteen and facing conscription. It is funny that Andy and I were considered a bit crazy, not for being wild, but for being so different from what was expected. One of the toughest guys in town with a nature-loving book nerd for a girlfriend, hanging with the rebels but not acting "right." Andy and I would walk by a small old farmhouse on Peabody Street and talk of raising a family there, how the house would be perfect. We were in our own dream world, but I was beginning to understand that nothing is free and only hard work gets you a home and a family. My parents taught their children well: love and dreams are nice, but they come with really hard work. But we could dream of that little house being ours.

Over the first few years I seemed to be a healing balm for Andy's tortured soul. His days in the reform school were not far behind him, and the physical scars were still visible. He seemed calmed by an intimacy that came with no expectations for performance. He could drop the tough guy exterior when he was with me. We did have sexual intimacy, it wasn't innocent like my first kiss with Mikey. It was just that our love making did not include intercourse; it was so much more than that. We would spend hours lying on the soft moss under a tree, far from people and prying eyes, and explore each other's bodies. Once a small wild rabbit hopped over to us and we held our breath as he just sat and watched us for a long time. It was a thing of beauty, as innocent and lovely as we felt our relationship was at the time. It seemed that we both felt that intercourse, fucking, inflicting the first pain of woman-hood upon me, may have destroyed the intimate and beautiful connection we had between us. It is not that Andy wasn't excited; he was very much so. Yet he respected my parameters, seeming to crave the loving touches and the comforting embraces that lasted so long we sometimes dozed off in each other's arms. I suspect he had never received much of that in his childhood, and neither had I. We truly met each other's mutual needs for love and affection for over a year.

The summer I was almost fifteen I had to take a job as a live-in nanny in Marblehead. I got to see Andy only one day a week and never at night that summer. I overheard many rumors that he was "screwing lots of girls from the neighboring town." The Middleton girls consid-

ered a group of Danvers girls to be rivals for their guys and it was probably true. There were a few skirmishes when some Danvers girls would
show up to brawl in Middleton, once outside St. Agnes church on CCD
night! Andy was gorgeous and could have had any girl that he wanted,
and for whatever he wanted them for. His testosterone was in full gear
and he didn't want another relationship, just sex. He never admitted it
and I never asked him directly, but whenever you start hearing a lot of
rumors, there has got to be some fire along with the smoke. He also was
becoming close friends with a local guy who dated a Danvers girl; we
started going out with this couple a lot. Not that sitting in Joe's beat-up
pickup in the square could be considered a date! I began to smell pot
on Andy's clothes and we just sat around in Joe's truck. I just knew they
were thinking that if dorky me weren't there, they could light up. As for
me, I still wanted to run in the fields, hide out in the woods, and have
picnics on the lake!

Another incident during the summer on my one day off put a bit of
a scare into me. I was worried that Andy was getting involved in more
dangerous pursuits. I was waiting at Richardson's Dairy when a convert-
ible pulled up and two guys, in their late twenties, called me over. They
told me that "Andy is waiting for you in the square and wants us to
give you a ride to meet him there." I thought for only a moment before
jumping in the back seat. After all, how would they know I dated Andy
if they didn't know him? They stopped the car halfway to Middleton
Square and one guy turned around and asked how old I was. I told him
fourteen. They looked at each other and the driver said, "She is kinda
young." Just as the passenger reached back toward my knee I leaped over
the side of the car and ran all the way home. Andy swore that he didn't
know them or their car, but that they might have heard me say goodbye
to him in the parking lot earlier. I don't think so!

My nightmare of a job that summer had instilled in me a huge
conviction that I would never again let people treat me with little respect
and as subservient. I knew I had to get a good education and I was ready
to move on! Andy and I saw each other for almost another year, but I
was also working hard in school and preparing to get my learner's permit
to drive. I wasn't much fun for Andy, as our dates had dissolved into he

and his friend and girlfriend smoking pot; I didn't smoke anything and was unwilling to have sex—a real dud for a date! I also knew that I could not get into any trouble as my parents were struggling with severely defiant behavior from my older sister. I had to be the good child! When I got my license and a weekend night job checking coats at the Country Squire Inn (later the Stephen James and then Angelica's restaurant), I felt strongly independent. I bought an old car for eighty dollars and had a job to pay for the car as well as the insurance. My father and I painted the huge 1959 Ford Fairlane together in his garage. I also facilitated all the arrangements for the junior/senior prom for my high school as I had connections where I worked. My cousin Joanie had Andy's brother as a prom date; he wore his military uniform and Andy wore a white tuxedo, making us stunning couples. Andy was the most handsome mystery man at the prom, and so many classmates wondered about just who I was. After the prom, I realized that Andy probably wasn't going very far in life and he wasn't the same fun person anymore. He had no ambition to get a job or a driving license. I broke up with him, but it wasn't a simple and quick thing. He still loved me, but I had changed and wanted much more than gorgeous looks. I could see beyond his looks and I didn't even recognize this new version of Andy. He looked intensely dangerous and scared off any boys who tried to date me. He suspected every boy of wanting me, even threatening the car valet boys in the parking lot of the restaurant where I worked. I didn't want to date, being so involved in making a life for myself. I finally wore him down by not giving him anybody to fight with.

A few months after last seeing him, I felt obligated to go to his father's wake after his dad passed on. When I left the wake, Andy, stoic and unemotional in the reception line, ran and jumped in my car as I drove off. He proceeded to cry hysterically over all that he wished his father had been, hanging out my car window and sobbing. I stopped and we held each other for a long time, until all his deepest pain had been released and he stopped crying. I dropped him off at his house and didn't see him again until over twenty years later. He drove up to the farm where I was living and raising my own family to pick up his wife, actually a relative of one of my brother-in-law's wives, and, evidently, they had several children. He still had the sculpted cheekbones that I loved and long black hair in a ponytail hanging down his back. He also had very bad teeth and looked very old. He looked out the window of his battered pickup and smiled at me, but then quickly went grim-faced. The dark eyes that I'd once admired as pools of emotion seemed not to see. I looked back; neither of us said anything and he drove off.

⚶ FIRST JOB, MOTHER'S HELPER ⚶

My parents expected all their children to get jobs by the time they were fourteen. As the minimum working age was sixteen, there weren't many opportunities. Although all four of us girls worked daily, almost exclusively hauling and stacking firewood, we got only fifty cents a week as an allowance. That would not even buy an ice cream cone at the dairy! We came up with a few other money-making ideas before we were fourteen. In late November, we harvested princess pine, a small woodland plant, from the local woods and made the most extraordinary wreaths, selling them for a few dollars each. I would have felt a lot worse about having taken so much princess pine, but all that land became a housing development in later years. In the summer, blueberry picking was a delight and actually got us enough money for the end of summer town picnic. The picnic was funded through the Mansfield Fund, a benefactor who wanted all of us poor Middleton children to have one out-of-town summer adventure. We still wanted some money for the arcades and food. We picked a lot of blueberries to sell at fifty cents a quart! Mom made it clear that by the age of fourteen, we would have to buy our own school clothes and needed to make "real money." Patsy, as the oldest sister, was the first victim! They found her a job as a mother's helper in what was considered an affluent area of Marblehead. As an adult, I visited this area and realized that, although presented as affluent then, it sure wasn't the old money oceanfront property that Marblehead is known for. I chuckle now at the simple split-level homes that the owners flaunted as "elegant." Patsy never said much on her one day off or even after the summer was over, but the next year she refused to go, and I was the next victim! Leaving my dear boyfriend of a year was really tough, but I think my parents thought this would be the break that would finally end our relationship. Patsy was becoming such a rebel that they used up their worries on her and really had no time for either of us. Both of our parents were working at the Parker Brothers factory in Salem at that time. I wonder if Patsy's experience as a mother's helper fed her need to rebel, as much as it fed my need to better myself with an education.

So, I was sent off to live with the same family my sister had lived with the previous summer. The mom wanted to spend her summer at the country club and not have to care for her one son. They had a most adorable two-and-a-half-year-old named Michael. I loved children and was excited that two of my girlfriends took positions in other homes in the neighborhood. We could take all the children we were responsible for to the parks together. I was looking forward to an exciting summer, even though I would only have eight hours off a week to return home. The father of the family owned a shoe factory in Lawrence, and his "sort of a limo" would take me along with three executives in suits and drop me off on Route 114 at the end of my street, picking me up on their return home. I got only one day off, and it was never a weekend day. I didn't get even one night to sleep in my own bedroom. In Marblehead, I had a drab room with a bathroom in the basement of their modern split-level home, with an intercom to the son's room so, although the parents were four feet away across the hall, if their toddler awakened, I was to come upstairs and comfort him. Those parents must have slept with a "white" noise machine or earplugs, not to hear their son crying or me comforting him. It didn't happen often, as I exhausted Michael with our fun daily excursions. As a fourteen-year-old I learned to sleep as most parents do, with one ear toward the baby's room!

I was immediately homesick after my friends quit their positions and returned back to Middleton to enjoy their summer. Susan and the others said they were not "going to be treated like dirt by these people." One lesson taught in my home was that you are not allowed to quit a job! My friends all said they had never been treated so much like poor, dumb,

farm kids while at the same time being told they should love the oppor-
tunity to live in such a nice place. I did enjoy Michael. I took him on
many trips to Devereaux beach, a long walk with him in the carriage. I
also, on my most homesick days, walked with Michael in the carriage
all the way to Parker Brothers' parking lot in Salem, leaving notes on
my parents' windshield saying, "I miss you." Friday was always a tough
night, as this was the only time the parents ate dinner with their son
all summer. Although told I needed to eat at the table with them to
help Michael manage his food, I was very uncomfortable as they said
prayers I was not familiar with. I was supposed to be invisible unless
Michael dropped his food or fussed. No conversation involved either
Michael or I, but the parents conversed throughout the meal. Only
at the end of the summer did they tell me that my older sister had
refused to join them on Fridays. I had never thought it was an option.
Although I thought I was mature for a fourteen-year-old, I did screw
up one night due to my intense longing to be around teenagers at least
once that summer. The family had left me with the children of a visiting relative for a week in addition to Michael, and I had finally got
them all down to bed and sleeping soundly. That was when I heard a
glorious sound, an amateur rock band practicing in a garage just one
house down. I listened from the screened porch and heard the sounds
of laughter from kids my own age. I don't know what I was thinking;
in fact, I wasn't thinking at all when I gradually walked down into
the yard to listen. I do remember longing for the lighthearted fun and
teen camaraderie that I had been deprived of all summer. I didn't even
realize that I had wandered to the edge of the property line, still in
hearing of the house but not in the house as I should have been. I didn't
get to listen long because I heard the voice of the woman that I worked
for screaming at me that I had left all those kids alone sleeping in the
house. I have never forgotten the lecture I got that night. I knew I had
made a big mistake, but I took a severe tongue lashing in front of the
relatives. I was mortified because I truly knew I had to be the responsible and mature child of my parents. They didn't fire me, though. They
knew they had a good thing, in spite of my one lapse of judgment that
night. In fact, after babysitting 24/7 for the three extra kids, the visit-

RAGAMUFFIN RISING

ing relatives gave me a gift of a cheap sweatshirt that didn't even come close to fitting. I acted humble and thankful.

I must mention my pay for the summer. It was ten dollars a week, and for those ten weeks I would make one hundred dollars. This was for six days and seven nights caring for a toddler, including making his meals and all other duties. I didn't have to do any heavy cleaning, as a housekeeper came in once a week. However, I did get a written scolding in letter form after I left some sand in the tub—the tub only Michael was bathed in by me! I always gave Michael a bath after our days at the beach, and my bathroom downstairs in the basement had only a shower. Seems the mom and dad were very upset at having a bit of sand in the tub, although I am sure they had another tub in their private bathroom. I never once ventured into their bedroom or bath, only steps away from the baby's room. On Friday night, after the special meal, the parents would play with their son for an hour. Otherwise, I was Michael's playmate and caretaker for ten weeks, and he would have a different teen every summer. I sometimes wondered about Michael and actually googled him recently, only to find he had passed on. I really hope he found love and warmth as an adult.

During the week, the Missus would go to some country club all day and into the evening. Her husband must have joined her there on weekends. They were almost never home in the summer except for Friday nights. She didn't have to shop because a company would deliver a rack of really nice designer clothes that she would pick from and then it would presumably be ordered in her size! During Michael's nap time I tried on those clothes, making sure to put them back on the rack in exactly the same way so nobody would know. I would like to think I developed a good sense of fashion; however, I knew I couldn't find any of these clothes in Zayre's or K Mart! My summer earnings of one hundred dollars had to buy all my school clothes, including shoes, so it wouldn't be designer clothes I would be buying.

I learned a lot that summer. The lesson I was supposed to learn, from my parent's perspective, was to know my place and follow orders well. My mom frequently told me that she had worked for a "rich woman" in her teens and was treated like dirt. "That lady I worked for would take a white glove and go over all the places I had dusted and make me do them again" was one of the memories she voiced to me more than a few times. Evidently, she wanted Patsy and me to have a similar experience. She wanted us to learn "our place." Mom would always remind us kids that we weren't like those rich folk. She reprimanded me if I called the evening meal "dinner," saying, "Do you think you're rich or better than us? Call it supper." My parents did not find it inspiring that I did want to be "better than us."

I flunked the lesson my parents wanted me to learn that summer. It was the best lesson I have ever flunked! I gave up an entire summer of my life for one hundred dollars. This was the summer that my boyfriend, Andy, became another person, a person who would always be my first love, but I knew it was going to end. I enjoyed my time with Michael and knew I loved children. I felt badly that he had such little contact with his parents—there but not there. I told my younger sisters not to ever take this job, as nobody should be made to feel of so little worth. I was insulted and belittled but left that experience with a new determination. In spite of my mother's and father's words of "wisdom," I vowed that I would never let people of greater wealth make me feel less important, less worthy of being treated with respect. I finished the summer with a determination to get a college education. I didn't know that would be received with such disbelief by both my parents and school officials.

❧ BOB AND LOUISE ❧

We didn't have relatives who visited us at our house very often. Uncle Eddie and Aunt Doe came over for special occasions, but it wasn't regularly. My parents did have a couple of very good friends though, Bob and Louise. Bob worked at Parker Brothers in Salem and was much younger than my father; he'd been engaged to Louise for many years. My sisters and I loved having Bob and Louise come over every week. Most Saturday nights, except for the few hot summer nights we went to the drive-in as a family, we all enjoyed a very competitive game of bingo. We played using pennies, everybody putting a certain number into a small pot in the center of the table. The first bingo winner for each game won the pot. We all saved every penny we had and filled up our own jars just for bingo nights. Sometimes I remember playing Parcheesi, but bingo was our favorite game to play with Louise and Bob. There were lots of laughs with them, and we needed to hear laughter more!

A few times my mother had to have surgery. Bob and Louise would stay overnight with us kids; I think my mom felt my father would need the back-up! I know my father never did dishes, cooked, or made sure we had our Saturday baths, and so that was probably another reason. When I was a pre-teen my mother had sinus surgery. She came home from the hospital with a tube coming out of her nose, secured to the side of it with tape. She had to hold one of those curved plastic bowls under the tube so blood and yuck could drip out of it. Being a very sensory-aware person, I almost barfed every time I looked her way! That visual ranked right up there with her asking me to help her find the very tip of her finger in the coleslaw she had just grated. It was only a small piece of flesh and the blood in the coleslaw led my eyes directly to it. I believe she intended to salvage the coleslaw for us, so of course I told my sisters that mom's finger had been cut off in it! None of us were hungry for that side dish anymore!

After Mom's operations, we'd try to stay busy outside, just as my father did. After Mom's hemorrhoid operation, Louise proved to be a really good friend. Evidently, as Mom told us, a day after coming home from the hospital, packed with gauze and healing, she was to gently pull the gauze from her rectum. Louise was the only one to help her with that horrid task! My dad kept the saw running and we worked throwing that firewood into the bulkhead with lots of noise during that fiasco!

The last time Bob and Louise stayed at our house was when my parents asked them to watch over Patsy. She refused to go on a trip with us, by plane, to visit another set of my parents' friends living in Kentucky. It was the last time they stayed at our house. I think Bob and Louise married about ten years after that. My parents kept telling Bob that he would lose Louise if he didn't stop putting off their wedding. They did marry and had three daughters. Louise was experienced in raising girls after all those years visiting us, and I'm sure they were wonderful parents. I will always be thankful for Bob and Louise Blanchard's friendship with our family.

⚹ FIRST PLANE RIDE ⚹

I felt so rich and sophisticated. My parents were taking my two younger sisters and me to visit their friends in Louisville, Kentucky. The last time we visited, we traveled by car, Mom, Dad, Patsy and I, as the twins weren't born yet. Patsy wouldn't be coming this time. She adamantly refused. My parents' best friends, Bob and Louise, were drafted into staying at our house to supervise Patsy. We all knew nobody could supervise Patsy, but at least it would cover my parents legally if something happened. I believe Patsy would have liked it if my parents had tried a bit harder to convince her to come, and she was furious that Bob and Louise would be at the house to "babysit" her. My parents just wanted and needed a vacation so badly. They had never taken vacations without their children, and a trip with only three kids would be fun and relaxing. My mom could concentrate on caring for the twins, who were about six years old. I dressed nicely and packed my own bag.

The prop jet pulled up to the runway at Logan Airport and we went outside and up the stairs to board. The twins sat next to my parents and I was across the aisle—thank goodness, because not long into the trip Jeanne and Janet started vomiting. My mother became very upset, and my father was just plain embarrassed. I have never been able to tolerate the smell of vomit, so I remained across the aisle with my head in a book. Two middle-aged Catholic nuns, in full habit, sat a few rows behind us. One of them came forward and asked if she could help. Mom handed the two of them over to the nuns in a blink of an eye! They took both Jeanne and Janet back to their own seats, sat them in their laps and held the throw-up bags, comforting them for the entire trip. The twins were eventually fine, and having never been held and hugged like that, enjoyed the last half of the flight. My mom was happy, and so thankful she was Catholic.

The flight was exciting, but Louisville was a big disappointment for me. I remembered when I was only two or three visiting the same friends in a shack in the mountains with a rope bridge to cross over the hollow. Now they lived in a house, identical to hundreds of others, in the suburbs of Louisville. One tree per small house lot, flat ground, and very little greenery. It was a good thing I brought a few books to read. I was thinking that my father, with his favorite line, "What are the poor people doing now?" was feeling rich to live where we had woods, gardens, and space! When we returned home, Louise and Bob reported that they never saw Patsy, but they said they heard her coming in late each night.

❧ HOLIDAYS! ❧

I always loved the holidays. It wasn't about getting lots and lots of gifts; it was about getting a few presents that made us feel like girls. Presents were not in the budget, but we still each got a new doll from Santa. As my father worked at Parker Brothers, we also got to go to the company party. All the workers signed up their children so that the gifts we got were age appropriate. And much to my parents' and our delight, Parker Brothers bought the gifts from other toy companies. We didn't want games that our dad made; we had game pieces all over the place. For many years my father took the big barrels of discarded wooden dominoes, game pieces, Ouija boards, and any other burnable game parts to use in our home's wood furnace. At the company Christmas party, we got a really nice doll or toy! We hung our stockings every Christmas, and Santa filled them. One year, as we were getting older, we thought we would hang our longest thigh-high socks. Mom gave us a lecture about being greedy! As children we never got any toys, unless it was Christmas or our birthday. We found out later that Mom had to save out a bit of her grocery money every week for months before Christmas to buy us gifts from Santa. Dad would not have had Christmas at all, yet he seemed delighted that mom had made it happen every December. Our stockings were filled with a bit of candy, a few cheap toys, and oranges and nuts. We also had a nice roasted turkey and pie and cake for dessert.

Our Christmas tree was just a white pine cut from the woods around the farm. Each ornament made the branch droop to the floor; however, lots of that aluminum tinsel hid the many bare spots. As my mother had once worked at Sylvania, we had large round lights for the tree. After we had moved into our small house, we continued to have pine trees. Patsy and I were in charge for years. This was the rare time we worked well together, and nobody ever got hurt. Christmas will do that! We would trudge through the snow looking for a very full pine, as there were no balsams on our land. In our wisdom or lack thereof, we noticed the tops of very tall trees looked much fuller than the small trees. Patsy climbed very high and cut the tops off a lot of trees; however, when they hit the ground and we stood them up, they weren't full at all. Every year, we finally dragged home a white pine that was just okay in our eyes. When my younger twin sisters were about ten, they took over the job. They brought home the most beautiful balsam REAL Christmas tree! No questions were asked! They were then assigned the job every year.

Easter was a holiday for dressing up to go to church. We did color eggs, but I don't remember getting any Easter baskets or ever being told there was an Easter bunny. Maybe after my mother spent a miserable childhood raising rabbits to sell and eat, she didn't believe in any miracle bunny! We did get a new outfit for church; from head to toe, we were dressed with class! We got patent plastic shoes that you could see yourself in, hats either with wide brims or, when we were older, a pillbox style, a nice dress, and sometimes even a dressy coat to go over it all. Mom told Dad we had to be all dressed up for Easter mass!

When I was earning money babysitting, I surprised my parents with Easter baskets that I laid at the end of their bed. I cut down washed-out Clorox bottles, as we used a lot of bleach in our household of incontinence. Then I bought Easter basket grass and speckled malted-milk eggs, which my father especially loved. It was weird how it made me feel really good to do this, but I got little response; in fact, they seemed uncomfortable and hardly acknowledged the basket. I didn't mind. I saw my father eating those eggs that night and felt good.

The only other holiday moment I remember well was a particular Memorial Day. We were teens and it was a cherished day off from working for all of us, including my mom. My father decided that year, for the first time, to march in the Memorial Day parade with other veterans, wearing his Army hat. Well, the parade was at 9 a.m. and we slept in. My mother was busy catching up with household tasks as she was working at the factory those years. My dad stormed in several hours later, fuming mad. He was really upset that none of us had gone to watch the parade. That was the one and only time that my dad contributed to town events. I did feel really badly for him and put a lot of guilt on myself. In hindsight, I never rationalized that he had never once come to any of my school or sports events. I didn't expect him to. None of us realized that it was so important that we come to something he was doing and that it had meant so much to him. He was a veteran and he deserved our presence at the one parade he'd marched in. I still feel guilty.

⚡ TOUGHEN UP! ⚡

My father was an inventive man. I can describe some of the creative things he made only as "contraptions." These contraptions were not made for fun; they were made to make our work easier. My sisters and I thought they were fun! My dad started clearing the fields for pasture with an old Ford truck that had no cab, just a wooden box to sit on. It had a winch built on the chassis and he could lift and move large boulders. Another vehicle, the woods wagon, was a necessity. By cutting the roof off an old car and taking out the back seats, he made plenty of room for timber cut in the woods way down toward Picariello's pit. It was easy to drive, even for us kids. Our wood yard was across from the house, on the other side of the road and adjacent to our field that ended at the cemetery. We would also get loads of junk lumber, full of nails and sometimes wire that held the boards together. The huge table saw, about four feet in diameter, was run only by my dad. It had no safety features whatsoever. We passed the wood to him and he slid it into the blade. He was fast and we had to keep up with him. When the gasoline engine was running, we needed to work quickly. We would often step on nails, and none of us had work boots— real leather boots were expensive. We had cheap canvas sneakers with thin rubber soles. They were great for wading in the polliwog ponds, but not so good when you stepped on a nail. It was understood, as we learned well from experience, that if we fell down when working with Dad, his response would always be, "Come over here and I'll pick you up." The same went for stepping on nails.

One time, when I was about eight, I stepped hard on a piece of wood that was stuck in the pile. The nail was so long that it came out the top of my foot. I screamed for Dad and he yelled back, "Come over here and I'll pull it out for you." Thanks, Dad! I couldn't move, so before I lost my nerve, I stepped on the board with the free foot as I pulled my other foot up off the nail. I ran to the house and Mom, after seeing the rust ring it left, took me to Dr. Jones for another tetanus shot. We kids had so many tetanus shots it was ridiculous, but it seemed every puncture wound or cut involved something dirty or rusty.

My father got tangled up in some wire one day while he was trying to grab some wood himself, as the pile was such a mess we couldn't get the wood out fast enough. He caught himself, but his leg swung up and into the saw, the blade catching him right near the end of his work boot. We just stared in horror, and he did too. After no blood gushed from the boot, he shut the saw off and we all walked gingerly toward his foot. There were all his toes, inside the boot, but exposed, the sock cut off but all his skin intact! He was a bit upset about losing the toe of an expensive work boot, but considering what could have happened, we were extremely relieved.

It didn't matter if we didn't want to drive the tractor. We also didn't get much in the way of a lesson. "Get up there and drive" was my father's lesson. Driving the woods wagon was just like driving a car, but the Ford tractor was a bit more complicated. Patsy took out one nice Balsam tree in the back yard, ran over it with the tractor and chopped it off mid-height. It was actually a backyard decoration, the only one, so nobody was happy about that. I failed badly on a job my father entrusted me to do. The side yard was a steep embankment and growing from the bottom were large trees with branches that my father wanted to trim. His plan was for him to get in the bucket with the chainsaw, and I would drive to the edge of the embankment and lift up the bucket so he could reach the higher branches. Unfortunately for all of us, the gravel banking wasn't stable and started crumbling under the smaller front tires. The brakes didn't help as we tilted forward and, just as my father leapt from the bucket to the high ground, the tractor and I bumped straight down the side of the embankment. What a scary ride! He looked down at me from the high edge of the gravel and shook his head. I had time to catch my breath, telling myself to "toughen up," as he had to walk around to the far driveway that led to the bottom of this "pit." Without a word, he started to cut the trees down just enough so I could drive the tractor out the back driveway. There was no other way to get the tractor out of there, as it was wedged into the grove of trees. I was just glad he didn't have to cut the really large trees that held our tree forts. Dad didn't actually blame me, but I always felt it was my fault. But then again, it wasn't my plan!

⚛ I JUST WANTED TO BE OUTDOORS ⚛

My sisters and I had what seemed like a lot of time to play, especially in the summer when there was no school. We would do our required hour or so of "wood" every day, filling the bulkhead with firewood. After that, we were free, and with my French grandmother living in our house after her stroke, indoors was not where we wanted to be. When we were young, we stayed within a mile of the house and explored the woods and ponds. Often, I would go exploring all by myself. I absolutely loved being out in nature. To my sensory delight, I would spend hours in the shallow warm "polliwog ponds." The best ones were down a dirt road near what was called Picariello's gravel pits. They may have been vernal pools, as shrubs provided some shade at the edges, but I did not know that term at the time. The rocks in the middle were sunbaked and the almost lime-green grass in these pools where the frogs had deposited their eggs was beautiful. Barefoot was always my preferred footwear, colanders and small buckets my toys. Jeanne and Janet went to my favorite pools once and brought home so many tiny frogs that they filled an old washing machine tub in the backyard. My mother asked them what was so interesting about all those tiny frogs. They exclaimed in sheer amazement, "Every frog is stuck to another one and we have to pull them all apart!" My mother had them return the frogs to the polliwog pond so that they could restart their mating season!

We had the best swamp in the world, and it was within yelling distance of our house. It was actually a pond surrounded by a bog and wetlands, but we always called it our swamp. In the eyes of a child who loved nature and its creatures, it was heaven on earth. The hillocks of marsh grass were stepping stones for us children, and they took us into a secret world. It was a hidden and somewhat forbidden world. My mother would try to scare us away from playing in the swamp, but she never succeeded. She told me that the "sewing needles," otherwise known as dragonflies, would sew my mouth closed. I'm sure both my mom and dad would have relished the rare silence from me! I found the iridescent beauty of the dragonflies amazing and would let them set on my arm or knee so I could study them more closely.

My sisters and I were great engineers. We built many rafts to take us deeper into the swamp. Friends from the neighborhood usually flunked stump jumping, so we had to make boardwalks for them. There was always recycled wood for the taking from my dad's piles. The tall reeds and grasses hid nesting birds, and muskrats dove out of sight at the slightest provocation. We learned to be quiet and be patient. It was "their" world, and we were only privileged guests who would get to see what they would allow us to see. There was also the intimidation factor: the large northern black water snakes and snapping turtles did scare us, but that just added to the excitement. There was also one deep hole that we stayed away from in the summer but loved in the winter. We would lie belly down on the black ice over this hole and study what was down there. During the winter we would shovel paths on the ice all through the swamp. We created little rooms deep inside the swamp, with a room for each of us that we could decorate with nature. We often had a campfire somewhere on the ice, adding to the fun. Friends from down the street would sometimes join us on the ice, skating from "room to room" on our swamp. All this was done without any adult intervention. My mother would call out the window in the winter when supper was ready and darkness coming on. When immersed in the trees, old bulrush, and water-loving shrubs, we couldn't see far enough in any direction to discern if the streetlights went on. But we could hear my mom's yell! With red cheeks, we would finally go in out of the cold. Our skin would often itch when transitioning from the cold to our overheated house. Just about the time we would sit down to eat, we'd start to smell our wool mittens as they smoldered and eventually dried on the hot radiators.

As a teacher, I often had to recommend sensory interventions for children. I would have liked to just say, "Let them play in a swamp!" Our days were full of squishy, smelly, visual, auditory, and often even taste sensations. Nature provides feedback for all five senses and it is free. It is not virtual, it is real. It can be unpredictable, often requires problem-solving, and develops listening and observational skills in children. When I think about the school administrators who said we Blais children entering school were illiterate, I balk. I was "reading" the natural world as a child and that is education, although not the type that got us any respect from school staff. I lament the loss of curiosity about the natural world as "screen time" now dominates children's lives. I also mourn the loss of wild wetlands and fight to preserve what is left in my town. I attended a planning board meeting in my hometown about a plan to develop homes very close to and even inside some of the wetlands buffer zones. The developer actually asked the question, "What good is a swamp?" in his presentation. Only in the past thirty years, when land prices skyrocketed in my former farm town, has every piece of marginal land been developed. I wrote a story for the local paper sharing all the wonders, the beauty, and the ecological benefits of preserving the swamps, the bogs, the streams, and the rivers. It seems it didn't matter, as progress was measured in dollars.

My parents may not have been able to buy us books when we were young, but we had advantages that many children didn't and still don't. Most children only get to read about or see pictures on their iPads of the places we were exploring all on our own. Back then, people didn't hire a lawyer and litigate for damages if their child got hurt on your property, so we could take chances. We were rich in some very important ways! Unfortunately, the knowledge, the authentic learning, and the independent skills we gained were not recognized or much appreciated in the academic setting. In our school, we were the poor kids, the kids with callused hands and rough dry skin, and the kids without potential.

As a high school teen, I am standing next to our beloved swamp.
Throughout my childhood, in every season, it was a place of wonder.

☙ POP'S DRIVING RANGE AND GIRL FIGHTS ☙

A mixed group of kids hung out at the golf driving range. An older boy, Jerry, who worked there didn't mind us girls hanging around. He would even let us pick up golf balls with the retrieval tubes out on the range after it closed. It was next to Richardson's Dairy, and I had enough babysitting jobs all year that I could afford to buy a frappe a few times a week. Pop rented the place from Richardson's Dairy. He was a big jovial man who never bothered us; he sort of just tolerated us. He wasn't there most of the time anyway. I was hanging with some local girls, but I didn't really fit in because I was trying so hard to be a goody two shoes. I valued my virginity, and not because of any spiritual or religious reasons. I was just so sick and tired of boys expecting that a Blais girl would have sex with them. The term used most often back then was "put out"—not very romantic! I had made it through a three-year relationship with Andy without having sex, and I certainly wasn't going to give it up now. My sister was always trying to set me up with dates for the drive-in theater. At first, I thought it would be fun. Thank God I lived within walking distance. I only caught on after several close calls with the boys Patsy set me up with. They were expecting sex, and Patsy was working hard to be sure that happened, always giving my date and I the back seat and either disappearing or making out with her date. It wasn't hard to turn their advances down as they had no romantic script and, for the most part, were not attractive. One boy said, as he grabbed for my breasts, "Come on, be a sport." I was flabbergasted! However, they were the kind of guys I didn't want to anger, either. I knew my sister wouldn't help me, as she set the dates up. So my famous line (in my own mind), was "I need to use the bathroom first." And home I would go, just a short walk up South Main to my street. Wow, did those guys need some lessons in courting a woman. In all the books I was reading, sex came only after romance, after the woman was dined and sent love letters. In the books I read, the handsome and muscled main character would have "loins burning" after he'd lusted after the woman's bare ankle for months. Historical romances were becoming my favorite books to read. I could wait for my own knight in shining armor.

I also flunked smoking and drinking. I couldn't stand the taste of beer, and the few times I tried smoking, I got so dizzy and sick that I couldn't stand. Maybe I should have tried harder. The one thing stopping me was my obsession over always being in control. I was an observer, and I couldn't observe if I was under the influence of anything. I took pride in my reputation, although I'm sure everybody else thought that I was living the fast life. After all, I was a Blais girl, and nobody expected anything different from any of us. The townspeople were wrong about many of my cousins and about me. Even without social media, stories spread fast that were often not true at all.

A former friend started a lot of rumors when I began trying to end our friendship. I did lose control one day, and it still amazes me. She was sitting with her younger sister and a few other kids on the rock wall separating the driving range parking lot from Route 114. I went up to her and asked, "Are you going to keep spreading rumors about me?" She smugly looked at me and said, "Yup," with a smile. At that point, I sacrificed the frappe I had just bought at Richardson's Dairy. I could never bring myself to hit anybody in the face, but a frappe in the face seemed justice for a person smearing my reputation in town. But she was a fighter! She jumped up and attacked and I had to fight back. Trying to stop her, I grabbed at her blouse and the entire thing ripped right off her skinny body. She was going for my hair, but I didn't let that happen. I kept flailing in her direction, keeping her long arms from getting a grip on me. Pop heard the cars blowing their horns and people yelling as we were actually on the road by then, one half-naked girl covered in frappe and a crazed, thick-haired girl with a shirt in one hand flailing away. We must have been quite a sight! Thank God they didn't have cell phone cameras back then! Pop ran over and jumped between us; it was all over in a few minutes. We each went our separate ways after I gave her shirt back to her. She and I became friends again, she did stop spreading rumors about me. We had some fun times. However, the friendship was really over a few years later, when she threw up in my precious first car. That was unforgiveable!

🌿 ALMOST CAUGHT 🌿

We went every Saturday summer night to the Middleton Drive-In. For teenagers with unlimited energy, it didn't stay open late enough. If somebody had a car, we would all venture to a hamburger place on Route 1 just after leaving Route 114 in Danvers, heading southbound. It was called "Duchess Burgers," but I don't know if it was part of a chain. Hamburgers were nineteen cents, so five of us could eat for a under a buck! They also had incredible ninety-nine cent frappes, although I don't think they were made with real milk. If nobody had a car on a given night, we would think of other things to do. This particular night, I was hanging with the Middleton kids who were considered "tough," But not the really tough thugs my former boyfriend Andy was hanging with now. I was comfortable with this group and they let me join them, even though I didn't smoke. Paradise Park kept trying to improve itself by adding more fun things for kids to do, other than drown in the manmade pond. This summer they had installed one set of carnival-style swinging cages, totally people powered. About fifteen of us had this great idea and off we went. We jumped the chain-link fence and ran for the cages. I was lucky that my partner was Jimmy D., who was sober as a judge. We got our cage swinging overhead before anybody else, so I was up high enough to see the blue lights immediately. I yelled "Cops!" but most of the others were laughing and screaming loudly, trying to make their cages go. They didn't seem to hear me. Jimmy and I got our cage stopped and ran for the back fence on River Street. The cops had to unlock the gate to drive the cruiser into the entrance, but still the other kids didn't seem to catch on to what was happening. A few must have escaped out the other way before the cops got in, because all the kids taken into custody fit into the one cruiser. Jimmy and I ran for our lives.

For me, it really felt like I was running for my life. I could see my parents' disappointed faces if I were the one sitting in the police station, Chief Wentworth's house. I could hear their sighs of frustration. They would have been devastated! I was the good kid; I could never do anything wrong. They had enough worries and tension trying to control Patsy. I had to be good. They depended on me to be the one they didn't have to think about.

Jimmy and I ran through the tall grass in the fields, coming out on Oak Avenue, a little side street off Haswell Park. We raced up the street, then slowed to walk calmly as we approached South Main. We sat on a rock that jutted out on the ground near the DiGiacomos' fence on the corner and watched the road, me finally letting the air fill my lungs again. As the cruiser slowly went past, with a full back seat, we just stared. That was so close! Jimmy headed home to Forest Street, and I walked slowly back to my house, silently saying a prayer of thanks. It was a night to remember and a lesson learned. It was safer if I just kept my head in a book! Wild and crazy fun was for those who didn't have their heart set on going to college.

⚹ MY SECOND JOB ⚹

I was fifteen when I got my next job, and it was a real job. Massachusetts must have issued temporary work permits or special summer permits. As my birthday was in October, I was a year younger than most of my classmates at school. Without wheels, my job opportunities were limited, and I had ambitions of making enough money to buy a car and have it ready when I got my license. With driver's education, we could get our licenses at fifteen and a half.

Just down the street was a good friend of my mom. Mary, a Russian immigrant, professed to have a good job in a shoe factory in Wakefield and was willing to get me in for the summer. A bit skeptical after the previous summer's job, I accepted with quite a few concerns. Copley Shoe was not as large as the giant Evans factory, but it had many floors and seemed huge to me. The town of Wakefield has a shoe on its town seal, in the early days of the 1800s, shoemaking was an important local industry. By 1869, nearly 60 percent of boots and shoes made in the United States came from Massachusetts. By 1913, children under fourteen couldn't work in shoe factories; it was the onset of child-labor laws. I was fifteen so I could work there, but I had my anxieties about it. My mom and dad were excited that I finally got to work in a factory; I think they hoped I would love it. They were very wrong!

I rode every morning with Mary and her sister Olga to Wakefield, about a half hour on the back roads. I was placed on the same floor as them, but not within sight or hearing distance in the huge brick shoe factory. Just as it was one hundred years ago, women worked lighter jobs than men, such as stitching and finishing. An assembly line (a two-foot-wide leather belt) brought shoes to the twenty-plus workers sitting facing forward at a single table to the side of the belt. Mary was skilled on a sewing machine, so she sewed leather in a different area, working quickly and doing "piecework," which brought higher pay. I had no skills whatsoever! Hence, I had to glue soles onto shoes—a very smelly job! They were very nice shoes, dressy heels made of fine leather.

I noticed right away that I was a bit different from most of the workers. I was really scared riding on the platform elevator with men who stared and talked in other languages. Wow, there were so many other languages. The message was the same though: I was way out of my comfort zone, and they all knew it! There were no walls on the filthy elevator platform, but I stayed near the side of the moving floor and never made eye contact with anybody. Work was hard and dirty, with strong glue and leather smells clogging my nose for eight hours a day all summer. I started getting nasty looks from other women on the assembly line when my crates of shoes were sent down the belt. It seems I was getting the easier soles to glue, and that was obvious to all. In my few trips to the disgusting bathroom, if you can imagine glue, dirt, and grime everywhere, including the toilet seats, I was smiled at by the foreman in charge of sending the workloads down the line. Seems he liked me, and that's why I was getting the better shoes. With a name like "Babe," he was clearly different from most foremen, but I didn't trust him! I felt in real danger by midsummer and didn't even go to the bathroom alone anymore, holding it until lunch when Mary would join me. The other women really resented me getting the easier shoes, although I was so slow that I never got up to making the extra money most of the other workers did. These women depended on speed to make enough money to live on; only with piecework numbers did your salary move out of the minimum wage range. In August, I found out that the foreman who liked me was really a middle-aged woman who wore men's clothes and taped her chest to look more like a man. This may be commonplace now but was quite rare and shocking in the late sixties. For a Catholic country girl, it was really hard to comprehend. I was growing up way too quickly!

The only good part of my factory job was that on the trip to Wakefield I saw a 1959 Ford Fairlane on the side of the road with a "for sale" sign on it! It was eighty dollars, and I knew I would make enough money to buy and insure it with my shoe factory earnings. It kept me going! I learned to work hard, just as my parents wanted. Mom had spent her younger days at Sylvania and then married and had children, only to return to a factory for a few years when we were older. Dad had worked in cotton mills and then spent the rest of his entire working life at Parker Brothers. With a fifth-grade education, he didn't have many options. I spent ten weeks in this shoe factory and never ever wanted to work in a factory again! I wasn't saddened when, years later, I found this factory had burned to the ground, having been abandoned when cheap shoes started coming over from China. The Trade Expansion Act of 1962 was bringing in more imported shoes. The Women's Dress Shoe Workers of Copley Shoe signed a worker's petition for adjustment assistance but lost their case with the US Tariff Commission. The decision was that "imports were NOT a major factor causing unemployment of workers at Copley shoe." I had worked there and I knew cheap imports could not compare to the fine leather dress shoes I glued soles on. The dress shoes that were made in Wakefield were selling for $22 at the time, with imports selling much cheaper. In 1973, Copley Shoe Co. signed a Trade Reform Act. I don't know if that helped, but it seemed as if all the shoe factories in Massachusetts were coming to dire ends! Suspicious fires were burning most of them to the ground by the time I graduated from college. Although I didn't ever want to work in a factory again, I felt bad for those who depended on the jobs, and those who had few options or who'd listened to "educated" people tell them they had no potential beyond factory work.

Then again, I had learned the lesson that stayed with me. I wanted a college education! My parents were beginning to accept that fact, although often voiced that I thought I was too good to work in factories as they did. The school officials at Masconomet High School found it even more difficult to accept. But I didn't listen to them either.

❧ MY FIRST CAR ❧

I'm not sure if anybody else thought my 1959 Ford Fairlane was cool or not. It was already ten years old, but it ran fairly well. The price was eighty dollars, and it looked a bit needy sitting on an embankment near the shoe town of Wakefield. But I knew working all summer at the factory that I would make enough to buy, insure, and fix it up a bit. I soon found out that it would serve as the vehicle that could hold the most kids to get into the Middleton Drive-In! When the admission was one dollar per carload, it served us very well. It was also the catalyst that brought my father and me a bit closer as we painted it in his garage. We studied the finished metallic green paint job with close scrutiny, trying to scrape off the one mosquito stuck on the shiny painted fender. We did it together and it just felt right!

All was good with the car for a while. It got me to and from my evening job at the Country Squire Inn, the largest restaurant and function facility in town. I checked coats late into the night, usually getting out at 1 a.m. Often I would work the front restaurant and I learned not to see or hear too much. Once the owner actually came in to help, and when he leaned over, I could see a revolver holstered inside his suit jacket. The owner didn't live in Middleton. There were a lot of rumors circulating about him, one about a mysterious barn fire at his home in which some young people died, evidently having seen too much. I saw nothing, ever! Sometimes I would work the humongous ballroom coat-check room. It had an automated coat rack that traveled into the next room and around back to me when I pushed the button. To my distress, it was built a bit too close to the wall in the back closet, often making thick furs fall off the rack way out back. Can you imagine, as a sixteen-year-old, having a couple give you the tag for their mink, and when the rack comes around, the hanger is empty? I would crawl back there and have to drag the coat under the racks and hand it to the very upset owner as I discreetly dusted off the cobwebs! Not a way to get a tip. Coat-check girls like myself made decent money only when we got good tips, and some nights I made out really well, especially in the ballroom. The benefit of the front room in the restaurant was that there was always a big bowl of polished apples for the customers as they walked in—this place was very classy! When I had a long shift, I would indulge in those apples. A few times a customer would leave a doggy bag behind after dinner to go to the bar. If it was left behind and was practically untouched, like a baked stuffed lobster without even a fork mark in it, it made its way into my large purse to take home. Sometimes, eating was good! I justified this to myself by the fact that I had to smell it all night in the coat room, and the person could not have been hungry when sitting down to dinner. Plus, after drinking for hours, he didn't even know where he'd left his dinner! Never in my home would we have had baked stuffed lobster, and the Country Squire Inn had the best! The coat-check girls were pretty awesome too.

I would often give my neighbor a ride home when she worked a coat-check shift also. Nancy was only a year younger but often naive and too trusting. I tried to take her under my wing! When checking coats in the ballroom area, there was a lot of dead time while the event was going on. The bartenders, easily in their forties, were very sleazy in my opinion, but Nancy always thought they had the best of intentions when sending over cherry Cokes to us very young girls. They didn't, and we both grew up a lot that year. My instincts throughout life have usually been very good, with few exceptions, and we learn from those exceptions.

As a junior in high school, I was proud to drive my car to school, even though it was much older than most of the other student cars. I almost always got to school early, so I parked it in the first space of the parking lot; just one turn at the end of the ramp and I was in my spot! The ramp went down a hill and was paved nicely. It made for great memories of up-hill burn-outs, especially by seniors showing off their cars in the spring. My senior year car, a '65 Mustang, got in some good burnouts when driven by friends, but never when I was driving. I had an experience with my '59 that was memorable but not in such a cool way. I was called out of class, after having arrived early, and told I had to go to the parking lot. The ramp was slick, may have even been icy, when Dave Smallman lost control of his very cool '64 Chevy Impala. As it plowed into the very large front fender of my very heavy iron Ford Fairlane, it pushed the other side of my car right through the side of the '63 Corvette that David Burke had borrowed from his older brother. I am not sure if David cried, but it was the saddest thing I ever saw. My car's big front end stuffed through a gorgeous Corvette. Just so sad. Dave did not get into trouble; he wasn't driving recklessly. I did not get into trouble; I was well into my parking spot and not even in the car. David may have been the only one who got into trouble—with his brother—but it wasn't his fault either. I hope his brother went easy on him and had good insurance! Dave and I recently laughed about this at a reunion, and he told me to be sure to use his full name and that it was a 1964 Chevy Impala!

I had to get rid of my car because of one of my friends. It wasn't her intent; she just didn't know that I have never had any tolerance for the smell of vomit. My strong olfactory sense helps me with remembering experiences of my childhood. Unfortunately, I remember smells like they were just yesterday. Just thinking about vomit makes me want to vomit! Would it have been so difficult for her to just hang her head out the window at the drive-in? I bleached, scrubbed, perfumed, and even tried to cover it with an afghan, but I could not get rid of the smell of vomit in my back seat. I could smell it from the front seat and could not live with it.

I sold the car to my cousin Roger, hoping he would appreciate the nice paint job and new tires. I charged him the same eighty dollars I paid for it. Within a few days, after a night of rowdy fun in Picariello's gravel pit, the car was burnt to a crisp. The gravel pit was just past the Blais farm down a dirt road that eventually turned into a nice trail out to Boston Street. It was big enough to have a small sandy track with hills that junk cars could jump over. Did I say I loved my cousin Roger? I did, but you could love Roger and still be totally infuriated with him at times!

When the car finally got stuck, he and his friends torched it for a bonfire! I'm glad I wasn't there, but I went to look at it the next day. The sight of those melted tires made me cry! His friend Fran was also to blame. I can't believe I took those two on a road trip in my new 1965 Mustang soon after! Sometimes I forgive way too quickly.

My 1959 Fairlane was already ten years old, but the price was right!

✧ "LES FLEURS DU PRINTEMPS" ✧ AND THE VIETNAM WAR

"The Flowers of Spring" was a perfect name for a junior-senior prom held on May 30, 1969. Saying it in French just made it even more special! The Country Squire Inn, located on the major route through Middleton, was where I worked; hence, I became the primary student organizer for the event. The only thing I didn't choose was the music—Don Richards and his orchestra. I think this group of musicians came with the package offered and the faculty members were delighted. Typically, most of the Middleton kids who were not in the college-bound or athletic groups, thought of as being on the fringes of polite society, did not attend the prom. That year we actually had a full table of couples. None of our dates were in high school. Either they were old enough to have graduated, had dropped out, or, like most of them, were heading to the Vietnam War. This is most likely why we felt comfortable sitting at the table off to the side in the bar area; seems all the tables actually inside the function hall were reserved. The school chaperones were very happy we were out there also. My name was never mentioned as having arranged the entire prom!

In 1969, the Vietnam War reached a peak in the amount of our young men sent into battle: 549,000 were shipped overseas into the war, an increase that was hard to comprehend and sent some draftees running for the Canadian border. Some people with affluence found doctors to state they were deferred due to ailments such as "bone spurs in the feet." I don't have any data to support this, but I would venture more boys went to college during the Vietnam War than in most years. However, college was not an option for every high school student. The others did their duty and either enlisted or obeyed the draft notice that summoned them. I was never proud of the war or the reasons we were there, but I always supported our "boys." On January 31, of 1968, 246 were killed or mortally wounded as the Viet Cong and North Vietnamese Army launched what was called the TET offensive. This seemed to be the incentive to increase the forces sent into battle in 1969. In the year of our prom, 11,616 boys were killed while fighting this war. These numbers should never be forgotten. They represent young people who will always be boys to me; so young, so energetic, so excited to become adults.

The law was finally changed to enable them to vote at the age of eighteen, giving them one privilege of adulthood. Congress, succumbing to the activists chanting an original World War II chant, "Old enough to fight, old enough to vote," passed the Voting Rights Act of 1970. If they were old enough to be drafted into a war where many would lose their lives, they were certainly old enough to vote. Early in the war, in 1967, we lost a young man, Jimmy Melvin, from Boxford, and we have never forgotten how young he was and the great sacrifice he made. Boxford was one of the three towns that sent students to our high school, and his family was well known and respected. His death was felt deeply; Jimmy and thousands of others never got the chance to vote in the country they defended with their lives.

I am so relieved that I purchased a cheap camera during my teens and documented some of the events of my life. It is hard to imagine that prom photo opps were not a big deal with many parents in 1969, at least not with the crowd I was with. In these current times, the photos are almost as important as the prom itself, with high school prom-go-ers having to plan hours before the event for elaborate photo shoots. I had somebody use my camera to get a few pics of Andy and me as we waited to ride with my cousin Joan and Andy's brother Jimmy. I took one picture of our table during the meal; I wish I had taken many more. We all looked so spectacular! Some of us went out into the main ballroom to watch the newly crowned prom queen, Betsy Myers, with her date, Birdie Bolten, by her side. I was very happy and fully supported the choice, even though I was also rooting for my field hockey teammates, Colleen and Chrissy!

The prom was the last big event of the school year of 1969. Just a week later, on June 8, Nixon withdrew twenty-five thousand troops from Vietnam. Although the war was not over, some of the draftees were sent to places such as the South Korean border, protecting it from North Korean forces. On June 3, some of the college-bound seniors were watching the last episode of "Star Trek" on television. Others were receiving their draft notices. That summer, "Woodstock" would become a household name, the Manson murders would dominate the news, and the Stonewall Riots would bring gay rights issues into our homes. I was remembering the prom and singing to myself the popular tune "Where Have All the Flowers Gone?," written by Pete Seeger in 1955 but popularized by Peter, Paul, and Mary in the sixties. The summer between my junior and senior years was one of both unrest and unity. It included protests against the war, not knowing what to believe from news coverage, and also a sense of unity among young people, a sense of trust, a sense of belonging to a social subset most often called hippies. Just as I didn't fit in with any particular group, I also wasn't quite a hippie, not in high school. I was much too conscientious of being in control and I needed to earn money. I had been raised to know that hard work was the way to success.

*You are cordially invited
to attend
"Les Fleurs du Printemps"
The Junior and Senior Promenade
of the
Masconomet Regional High School
Friday, May 30, 1969
at Country Squire Inn, Middleton
Russell's Orchestra*

I was so proud to organize the prom that I didn't need recognition from students or staff. I knew I had done a good job.

Andy looked absolutely magnificent in his tuxedo. He was the mystery man of the evening!

☙ STRAWBERRY FIELDS FOREVER ☙

The summer after I graduated, August 1970, was a memorable year for many very sad reasons. It was also a year of freedom, restlessness, and a celebration of life. The Vietnam War gave all young people a sense that life could be over at any time. Many of us lost friends in a war that was more divisive to the nation than any other conflict. Even during my early childhood, when we were given lessons on how to survive nuclear annihilation, we always felt as if we were in control of our fates. Now we were fighting a war that we did not understand, the press confusing us even more with stories of our soldiers killing women and children. I did not have any friends who ran from their duty to Canada; however, there was an event l was excited to attend, and it was over the border.

The hippie days were days to live life as though there was no tomorrow. I wasn't quite as free as that, being fully invested in getting into a college. I did want to travel and have a few adventures before starting my higher education. I had missed Woodstock, but another rock festival in Bowmanville, Canada, at the Mosport Park raceway grounds, gave me a yearning to let loose. I was seventeen, but I had new wheels and was ready for a road trip. I also wanted to see Niagara Falls. The tickets were fifteen dollars for all three days. My mother insisted that I would be safe if I took along my cousin Roger, and he then invited his friend Fran to come along too. My parents had no worries. They should have!

My really cool 1965 Mustang was dark green with a hard top. It had nice bucket seats and a beautiful interior. All that was lost on my two immature passengers. Fran was antsy in the back, and Roger had incredible difficulty sitting still for over four hours at a stretch. By the time we got to Niagara Falls for our first sight-seeing excursion, he had already pulled out some wiring and other stuff from under the dashboard with his feet that just couldn't stay still. We roamed around the falls with Roger taking pictures on the trusty Polaroid camera that he loved. After expending a bit of energy, we were all set to get through the border for the rock festival in Canada. The Canadian Border Patrol, worried about patrons coming up for the festival, required each person to show that they had at least forty dollars on hand, proving that they could support themselves while in Canada. Some of the lines waiting had two twenty dollar bills being passed from person to person as they went through the line. Nobody pocketed the money; they discreetly passed it along! At the same time, people with cars had to park them off to the side where they were being inspected.

We arrived at the Strawberry Fields Forever rock festival in time to set up our tents in the big grassy field. The name came from the fact that John Lennon from the Beatles and Yoko Ono were supposed to perform, but they suspected the Royal Canadian Mounted Police was spying on them and they declined. When documents were declassified later, their suspicions were proven true. John Lennon wrote "Strawberry Fields Forever" in 1967, basing it on a special place he'd enjoyed as a kid in Liverpool, England. The location for the festival was changed after John and Yoko backed out, and there had to be some clever deceptions to get a permit for this festival. The new location was 11 kilometers east of Toronto, and we didn't have any trouble finding the fields. My Ford Mustang wasn't four wheel drive, but I managed to drive into the fields. Roger and Fran would have pushed me if I got stuck, so I wasn't too worried.

The event was much more highly promoted in the United States than in Canada. It was dubbed a championship motorcycle race with "contemporary entertainment." There really wasn't any race that weekend; that was just a ruse used to get the permit. Evidently the promoters of the event also wanted a carnival atmosphere, so they brought in a huge Ferris wheel. That night, just as the lesser-known rock bands started, a large crowd watching the Ferris wheel began screaming. Two bench-style seats on the ride had broken loose and the riders thrown to the ground underneath the wheel, their backs now being torn apart by the other chairs as they passed over them. Apparently, in a stoned state, most of the crowd just gasped, and nobody got to the Ferris wheel controls to shut it off for what seemed like a very long time. An ambulance finally made its way in and carried away the severely injured people. That was an inauspicious beginning to an event that could have been another Woodstock. An estimated 75,000 to 100,000 people attended. The music that night was great, but my heart wasn't in it, having visions of the injured people stuck in my mind. Roger, Fran, and I were not stoned at all, and that could have been our problem! Of course, I had to stay in control and make sure Roger and Fran didn't get in more trouble than they could handle.

The next day was really hot, actually blistering August heat out in the fields. I did enjoy Grand Funk Railroad and a few other really good musicians that evening. Alice Cooper and Jethro Tull also performed, and I especially enjoyed them. By the third day, the few water trucks provided for drinking water were sabotaged. Water poured out onto the grass, and naked sunburned people poured into the newly created mud hole. Roger ran for his camera! I just watched from afar, sitting in my tent on a knoll, as Roger started taking pictures, he himself fully clothed. Finally, someone pointed, and I heard, "Get the guy with the camera." Roger ran faster than I thought possible with about fifty naked people in pursuit. He returned to our tent in a few hours, still breathing heavily. I'm not sure what happened to his camera; he didn't have it and I didn't ask. I never saw any pictures from Strawberry Fields Forever! The event finished up with Sly and the Family Stone wanting to take us higher, but I was happy we all had an exciting three days without any serious incidents. My parents didn't even ask about the festival, being perfectly content thinking Roger kept me safe and sound!

It came with a loan payment book, but my 1965 Mustang took my cousin, a friend, and me across the border to Canada for a rock festival.

⚜ OH, WHAT A NIGHT ⚜

Near the end of my senior high school year, I met a young man in a Navy uniform who quickly stole my heart. We went on a few dates while he was home on leave awaiting deployment to Vietnam. The intensity of relationships with servicemen was immediate, as the outlook for return was grim. Although we grew up in the same town, I had not met this young man before I saw him in uniform and thought him handsome, worldly, intelligent, and intense. He was a few years older than I, with dark hair and dark eyes. The relationship didn't last even long enough to get a picture, but I will never forget our last night together. I knew that I would not have sex, as I strongly felt I might never see him again and didn't want to take any chances with pregnancy or STDs. We spent the entire night together at his brother's place, alone in a secluded room, on a couch, just snuggling and listening to "old" Johnny Rivers albums over and over. We talked of the war in hushed tones, kissed, caressed, and, off and on, we even fell asleep. It was a desperate sort of bonding, the type the young people in wartime must be satisfied with. He would have liked having intercourse, but the night was intense in every other way so it didn't seem to matter that much. At that time, I hadn't paid much attention to the Johnny Rivers songs, with the exception of "Where Have All the Flowers Gone?"—a much bigger hit sung by another artist a few years later. The Beatles had overtaken the music scene during my high school years. I had apparently missed the popularity of the Rivers songs as I would have been in junior high or younger when they were released. The song "Poor Side of Town" really resonated with me, as my entire town had been treated as the poor side during all my high school years at Masconomet. Johnny Rivers' music has stayed in my heart and this young man has also, although our relationship was sabotaged by both his cousin and the Vietnam War. After he left the next morning for deployment, I wrote to him often and he wrote back; this continued for a few months. His letters were full of horror stories and close calls. He was stationed somewhere in the Mekong Delta on Navy riverboats. On one mission he was called away for a phone call or briefing of some sort and missed his boat as it shoved off into the Mekong River. During that attack, every American soldier was killed. About the same time, I started getting letters in which he would accuse me of dating other boys, evidently as reported to him by his cousin, who was also writing to him. I was actually hanging in groups and not dating anybody but was not sitting home either. It didn't matter. After the close call with mortality and all he was seeing in Vietnam, the tone of his letters started to change. He was angry, raging at the war, the craziness, the confusion, and me. It didn't help that when these soldiers returned, they were treated with honor by some but distain and hatred by others. There were so many casualties of the Vietnam War, including those still alive and severely affected by the experience. I saw this soldier only once after he returned for an informal date. He was full of drunken anger at everything, ready to pick a fight with anyone at the least provocation. I have heard that he eventually settled in, married, and started a family but that the war had made some permanent changes in his outlook on life. I have no regrets about our very short romance. in my mind he will always be the handsome Navy man in my arms listening to Johnny Rivers songs all night.

≋ LOOKING BACK AT MASCONOMET ≋

Some will tell you they had the most rewarding six years at Masconomet Regional High School. Most of these were either athletes or the children of white collar working parents. Children of parents who served on school committees, donated to the football signboard, showed up to watch all their child's games, ran fundraisers for the band—these students often had a good experience. Middleton was in a transition from farming to blue collar workers making decent money in places such as General Electric. There were not very many doctors, lawyers, or highly paid sports figures, as there are now. The parents moving into Middleton wanted the best possible education for their children. And they wanted them to feel good about themselves.

I reached out on social media to those who wanted to share their experiences. Many told me that they still haven't fully recovered from their junior high and high school experience at Masconomet. When word spread that I was writing a book, I received emails that were so angry I could feel the emotion in the venomous words. So many wanted to share just how negative their own experiences had been. I chose not to print many of them, but I assured all that I heard them. Especially sad was that these memories were still so vivid. "Two Topsfield girls sat next to me and constantly reminded me of how unfortunate it was that I lived in Middleton, to be so poor and have to wear such shabby clothing." Another person stated, "My dad said they called Middleton people 'drunks,' but they all came to our town to buy alcohol." It must be noted that Topsfield and Boxford were "dry" towns, and to this day

Boxford still does not have one place to buy liquor. One person was still upset that a Masco principal sent her brother home because his hair was too long. He told the principal his parents didn't have a car running at the time, and they said "walk." He lived about six miles away on the far side of Middleton. This next comment was just too honest not to share: "I was told by the Masco guidance counselor that I was not 'college material.' I bought into this only to find out later that it was a huge pile of steaming bullshit."

All the comments I received, and there were too many to print, reinforced the general negative atmosphere that Middleton kids were immersed in. We dealt not only with low expectations, but the idea that the mere presence of Middleton students was impeding the progress of the much more capable and invested Boxford and Topsfield students. One said it very well and wanted it shared: "The wide gap in socioeconomic conditions was ignorantly exploited by myopic and snobbish school administrators at Masco."

I still love Middleton, so I stayed here, moving to another farm across town to raise my children after I married. They thrived on building forts, riding dirt bikes, swimming in the irrigation pond, exploring the swamps, and having the freedom to go off for the day with many cousins all living on the farm. My husband's younger brothers had severe learning disabilities and graduated Masco with diplomas exactly the same as the other graduates, even though they could hardly read or write. Although I am not a huge proponent of testing as a measure of ability, I am happy that students are not being passed from grade to grade anymore, without receiving the help they need to make progress. Massachusetts now has strict guidelines to ensure all students meet basic academic skills. My own children, with the same last name as my husband and having some of the very same teachers that we had over twenty-five years before, had many experiences that demonstrated a prejudgment of ability. In fact, a school psychologist, completing the testing of my daughter I had asked for, exclaimed to me with utter disbelief, "How could you possibly know the names of those tests you asked for?" I paused a moment and then replied, "I am a special education teacher with a master's in curriculum and instruction and test children regularly. I have high expectations for every one of my students and my own children. And I also talk regularly to your special education director as part of my job!"

I would like to say Masconomet became a less judgmental place to get an education. It has. Most of the recently hired teachers don't have any idea of the past and know Middleton only as an affluent bedroom community. I am also proud to say that a former student of mine is teaching there! However, it has taken too many years, and the change in the past fifteen to twenty years, unfortunately and most significantly, may have come from the influx of affluent people. It seems the mansions of the newer residents, now being built on all the camp lots and farmland formerly owned by the "townies," may be the primary factor in deciding that students are "worthy" of being college material. I hope that is not so, and I encourage some of the new proposals coming from recent administration changes. I would also hope that teachers see the potential in all students, regardless of socioeconomic background. With the influx of young and forward-thinking staff, I sincerely hope that educators, both at my former high school and at every school, try to find every student's gift and greatest abilities.

WOMEN OF THE FIFTIES AND SIXTIES

Thinking back on the many ways my mom acted, and the manner in which my sisters and I were treated by others, I realize just how different times were back then. It makes it easier to understand. Up until the Violence Against Women Act of 1994, it was routine for police responders, when made aware of a husband's abuse toward his wife, to look the other way. Domestic abuse was officially designated as a "private family matter." A wife was not allowed to refuse sex with her husband, so he was never charged with rape as long as the victim was his wife. It was much the same with child abuse. Everybody knew which children in town were being forced to work too hard and which children were actually beaten, but the authorities did nothing to stop it. Once, when we were young, a complaint was filed, but it was because, in the eyes of our teachers, girls shouldn't have calloused hands. I am sure the complaint had good intent behind it; however, it showed the belief that girls should not be outside doing physical labor, although boys certainly could be. My sisters and I never felt we were worked too hard, because my cousins were working much harder. My father did not realize that he was challenging gender stereotypes by working us like typical boys of the times. He just knew that he didn't have any sons to do the work! But the pride he had in his daughters' abilities to drive tractors, work independently, lift heavy loads, and/or figure out how to do a "man's job" was evident, and it gave us confidence.

The injustice of the way women were treated was reflected in my mother's stories, not just of her childhood, but of the time during her childbearing years. I thought my mother did not stand up for herself with doctors, until I did some research and found out women were not allowed to question doctors. In fact, the practice was to bring your husband with you and the doctor would talk with him about his wife's medical problems. It is preposterous to think a man would be able to accurately describe a woman's menstrual pain, and that the male doctor felt comfortable talking to her husband while she sat there like she didn't exist.

A woman could not get her own credit card until 1974. She had to bring her husband, brother, or father to co-sign. An employer could also fire a woman who got pregnant for no other reason than being pregnant. This made it much harder for a woman to escape an abusive husband—they usually had none of their own money, and because sex was not a choice, they were often pregnant. As I have said before, we grew up in the fifties and sixties but lived more like they did in the forties. Times were changing, but those changes were taking a long time getting out to our little farming community. The library was my window into the world, and I found an exciting newly published book in the late sixties. Betty Friedan's *The Feminine Mystique* was actually released in 1963, but I believe I was a senior in high school before I discovered it. The three careers a woman was expected to pursue in the fifties were wife, mother, and housewife. It was always thought that an "old maid" would be relegated to a teaching job. After reading *The Feminine Mystique*, I still wanted to be a teacher, but I would also be a wife, mother, and a bit of an activist in everything I pursued!

☀ EPILOGUE ☀

My father wore his teeth to my college graduation. It was only a two-year college, but I would return to school to get my bachelor's degree and eventually my master's degree in teaching young children with special needs. He and my mom were very proud, but they both seemed very uncomfortable in the collegiate setting and didn't stay on campus long. I had never been able to afford to live on campus, but I was there all day and every evening that I didn't have to work the many jobs required to pay for my books, car, and clothes. My father was not alive when I got my master's degree, but he was around to know I had a very fulfilling teaching job in my hometown, where both my parents were told not to expect any academic success from me. I honored Mrs. Lewis at a school ceremony where I was receiving a service and dedication award. She was my invited guest. I was thankful I got to publicly recognize her as she passed on a few years later; she was truly my academic savior.

My father passed on at sixty-eight, the result of years of smoking. My mom developed Alzheimer's, and during the time she regressed she would often talk of memories from her own childhood. Her brother did the same. My sister Patsy passed away from lung cancer at the age of sixty-five. We spent her last few months sharing our grandchildren on fun outings where she wanted me to take lots of pictures so that her grandchildren could remember her with love. My two younger twin sisters remain very close and are doing well. They both have exceptional talents in gardening and caring for their many rescued cats. They also are very physically fit, athletic, and have beautiful hair! We spend much time laughing together about our childhood.

After fulfilling my dream of getting a teaching degree and eventually a master's degree in teaching young children with special needs, I worked as an educational assistant in the integrated preschool that I lobbied to start in my hometown. I was distressed that the children in my hometown had to travel from their home community and attend school in nearby cities, often collaborative programs for children with more challenging disabilities. I also had worked in these programs while raising my own family, and without typically developing children as role models, the children did not have as much success as I knew they could have. Speaking at a town meeting, with Superintendent Fitzgerald also advocating to start an integrated public preschool, I faced many judgmental comments. The arguments for the town were financial— they would save a lot of money on transportation costs. Children who went out of town for their education rarely returned, so the town would fund thirteen years of public school for each child. But other public comments showed a lack of understanding.

As my family did respite on weekends with Al, a young man with Down syndrome who was non-verbal, some comments from the public suggested the program would include adolescent men with severe disabilities. My own pre-teen children loved Al as much as I did, and they were proud to take him to the town basketball courts, where he would shoot basket after basket without missing a shot. The town kids were amazed! Many parents, however, feared what they did not understand. After I explained that an early childhood preschool program would be only for children ages three to five, the proposal passed. When the program became so popular that we divided the classes into one class for three-year-olds and two classes for four-year-olds, I took the job as teacher of the four-year-olds.

I loved my job for twenty five years. Designing and implementing a curriculum that integrated modifications for learners with challenges was exciting. It had to be active, literacy-rich, and multi-sensory. I also included many outdoor nature activities and many special parent/child events, such as a "bear hunt" and a Thanksgiving dinner for all. It also had to meet the stringent state frameworks for Massachusetts Pre-K learning standards. My job also included parent meetings, writing educational plans, special education testing assessments, and behavioral plans with training for my staff. I had also worked at a state institution, Hogan Regional Center, during the years I was having my children, needing the great medical insurance they offered. This experience, as well as my years at the consortium, gave me unique abilities to teach children with behaviors that were often intimidating to regular education teachers. I taught professional development to teachers with a focus on de-escalation and classroom strategies to lessen behaviors that would reduce a child's chance of staying in public school. Interventions before age six, classmates exhibiting typical social and emotional behaviors, small class size, and very qualified teachers and instructional assistants is the key to success. In twenty-five years, fewer than five of my hundreds of students had to move to a more restrictive school setting after kindergarten. Many have achieved great success and they all still call me Mrs. R.

Because of the early years of my own schooling, I am passionate about preschool for every child being a federally funded mandate. There is Head Start for children of very low economic families living in the cities, and they deserve a good program. There is nothing for children who do not have special needs and have moderate-income parents struggling to get by. I was very upset when a child had to leave my preschool program because the cost was prohibitive, either because of a tragedy, an illness, or a loss of the parent's job. The lottery system for picking our typical students was extremely competitive. A child had to have two areas of disability to enter the program as a special education student. Children with autism, Down syndrome, cerebral palsy, and a myriad of other diagnoses would make up a third of the class. Children with severe language delays as well as the social delays related to this would be included as special education students. A child with only behavior difficulties would not qualify, even though I would advocate that early intervention was the best chance of remediation of these behaviors. Also, children at risk due to a lack of literacy at home, such as I had as a child, would not qualify. If a parent could not afford a good preschool, the child would enter kindergarten with a disadvantage. As most children in a town such as Middleton attend preschool or daycare, they develop the very important social and pre-literacy skills that kindergarten teachers expect. Kindergarten curriculum in my town has expectations that students can wait in a line, sit for a story, hold a book the correct way, and follow a classroom agenda. With small towns that have wide disparity in income levels, home values, and parental education, funded preschool for all would be an equalizer, almost as valuable as the public library!

I have time to write now that I have retired from an exciting career in teaching. My first goal was to share and hopefully inspire other educators to always believe in every child's potential. As my children attended the same schools that I did, I knew it was still a dream that all children would be encouraged to reach for the stars in whatever direction they felt drawn to. I am proud to say I believe that with this next generation, it is happening in most schools. But not all. Children of poverty, of other languages and cultures, and those with differing abilities are still being advised to proceed in a specific direction based on preconceived beliefs. I was most dedicated in my career, sometimes to a fault according to some administrators, to making sure every child had the best possible chance of succeeding within my class, within their hometown school, and within the community in which they lived. And no child in my class was ever told they could not use the bathroom if they had to go!

☀ ACKNOWLEDGMENTS ☀

My greatest appreciation to my husband and children. We have shared a life of love, supporting each other through the trials that life threw at us and celebrating the much greater joys we shared together. I moved through my life as a bit of a contradiction, just as I grew up! I wanted to be a traditional stay-at-home mom, so as to not miss one moment of my children's lives, but I also sought adventures, travel, and a fulfilling career. It all worked with my career as a teacher, having the same hours and vacations as my children. My family was also an integral part of my teaching, helping me with the many activities that made my career so much fun! Early on, my gratitude goes to my second-grade teacher, Mrs. Georgia Lewis. She saved my literary soul and defied her own administrator to start me on my path toward attending college. I thank the Flint Public Library in Middleton, the great equalizer for all in search of literacy! As we couldn't afford to buy books when I was a child, I have become a bit of a book hoarder. I love owning the books I read and continue to battle my reading addiction. The library is also a place where I feel welcome to present cultural programs about my travels of over thirty years to the Navajo Nation, water conservation, and sustainable living programs.

I also thank all the people who shared their experiences growing up in our small town; they inspired me to write this book. I was so lucky to grow up in a safe, rural town with an abundance of forests, fields, and wetlands to explore. There are still some beautiful woodland trails, our great Ipswich River for paddling, and dedicated people who try to preserve them. Thank you, old Middleton!

My deepest gratitude goes to the three people that I trusted to read my early stories. Pike Messenger, an author himself, gave me incentive to move forward, Linda Barthuli gave my story a positive and passionate review as only a best friend can, and Claudia Giustra gave me a unique perspective, having grown up in Camden, Maine, and deeming my story a bit "shocking." I appreciate all their advice and inspiration. Thank you to Indie Author Books and Christina, who was always excited and answered all my many questions. Maine has become my second home, as my children and grandchildren live there, and we all feel that central Maine reflects more of the childhood days for all of us! The years we loved!

I thank my parents with all my heart. I may not have grown up being told that I could be whatever I wanted to be—I was told just the opposite; however, I grew up strong, resilient, and confident! Once they saw my resolve, my parents paid for my first two years of college tuition, as a day student, which was a big expense for them. My parents did the best they could, and I learned from what I didn't have what I wanted my own children to have: not a big house or material wealth, but affection; hugs and "I love you" from me every day! Interestingly, when my mom was sinking into Alzheimer's, she would repeat back what we said to her. My sisters and I would say "I love you," and she would answer back, "I love you." It was so nice that we got to hear those words for over a year before she stopped speaking. I probably encouraged my children to go to college a bit too strongly but supporting them throughout their schooling came easily to me. My children and grandchildren will always be my greatest gift. I hope to share many more adventures with them. I thank them for keeping me young!

I am very thankful for my very rewarding teaching career and for all that my students taught me. Known as "Mrs. R" by over a thousand children, some with doctoral degrees now, I relish the fond memories they still share with me of all the fun we had in school. I know I made a difference, and there is no greater feeling! They taught me that early test results, early literary experience in the home, and learning challenges do not have to determine a child's future. When school staff truly believe in their students' capabilities, when they expose them to the wonder of reading and the value of curiosity, and when they provide the extra support students need to jump the hurdles, amazing things can happen.